Direct Awakening in Meditation

From Mindfulness to Knowingness

Direct Awakening in Meditation

From Mindfulness to Knowingness

Shree
Sherrie Wade, MA

ISBN: 979-8-89686-693-0 (softcover)

Cover design: Sherrie Wade (Shree) and Laurie Tunis
Cover photo: Ellen Reitman (Gyaan)
Interior book design: Sherrie Wade

Published by Sherrie Wade, Boca Raton, Florida, USA www.transformationmeditation.com

Printed in the United States of America
First printing edition 2025

Disclaimer: The practices and methods expressed in this book are derived from the ancient system of yoga philosophy. The techniques are gentle and meant for you to experience peacefulness, ease, and contentment. If at any time you feel uncomfortable, please stop practicing. Please check with your doctor or therapist before beginning these practices or if any problems arise. We are not responsible for the misuse of these techniques. They are not to be performed while driving a vehicle or operating machinery or at any time when you are not of sound mind.

Direct realization takes place when all the waves or rays of attention become immersed into the fourth state of consciousness. This state is aways there, but it reflects in the ordinary human system as three states of consciousness: waking, dream, and deep sleep. In the fourth state, it is not the mind that realizes. The real Self realizes by itself.
Swami Shyam, *Raj Yog.*

This book is dedicated to my Guru-ji, Swami Shyam (Swami-ji), with whom I had the privilege of studying directly with for forty years. He lived in the fourth state of consciousness, the direct awakened realization, all the time. He showed, through his presence and unending expression of this knowledge, that we are that same Being, forever pure and true. Through this direct awakening, we know that we are also that realized One.

Table of Contents

Introduction

My purpose in writing this book is to consolidate many enlightening articles I wrote over forty years, based on sessions with my teacher, Swami Shyam (We affectionately call him Swami-ji or Guru-ji). I had published many of these articles that I put into the chapters of this book as they address critical topics of his teachings. They can help you to systematically understand this knowledge. They include lessons based on the questions in Satsang (the daily yoga philosophy session we had with Swami-ji). Swami-ji answered many students' inquiries. Since the questions are similar to the ones, we all have, they may be answers to your questions, too. His expression is unique and spontaneous and leads you to his enlightened vision, which is a direct awakening of your true Self.

Swami-ji translated and wrote commentaries on many yogic scriptures and spoke endlessly to many international students. His exalted and unprecedented teachings are revolutionary and practical as they suit the modern world. He often said that you don't get to freedom from bondage and that he is creating masters and not disciples. He never required a set schedule or routine. He once told me that I was like Bharati, who took Shankaracharya's teaching from his numerous commentaries on these scriptures and wherever they could use clarification for the modern world, she did that.

Swami-ji was a visionary when he told me this, but I didn't fully understand what he was referring to. I was teaching meditation classes in the West then and clarifying and simplifying his message to my students, so that is what I thought he meant. Now, I find that his vision was vaster than I had thought.

Later, I wrote articles and books and recorded audio and video talks on his teachings. These were to help those who wanted to concisely hear or read about his most pretendant lectures, commentaries on the yogic scriptures, and the numerous talks he gave with his enlightened knowledge.

Swami-ji usually spoke and wrote to more advanced students, although the teachings apply to anyone open to practicing them. He spoke and wrote only to unfold the Vision of Oneness, which sometimes boggles the mind until it releases you into its freedom through one's own direct experience. Swami-ji said to use your mind to do your work but then leave it on the coat rack when you come home to your own Self.

Swami-ji showered us with so much knowledge for so many years through his direct experience. I want to show you this path to your awakening in a precise and easy-to-understand format so you can begin to have your own direct experience. To have a direct awakening through meditation is the only way to have the knowledge that remains with you. In your direct awakening, confusion and trouble cannot remain.

Sometimes, you may forget and fall back into limited human consciousness and existence as only a body, mind, and senses. Forgetting your true nature is not your fault, as it is the human condition you have practiced. However, direct knowledge will always be there, too, because now you have experienced it and know it directly. The mind can't fully grasp this knowledge but studying it can take you into it. Swami-ji would often say that you are already that Pure Self, so you can't ever really lose it; you are it. The power which allowed you to forget is your same power with which you can remember.

The purpose of this book is to make you aware of who you are as the highest Self. Nothing else permanently exists as it changes, just like the pictures on the TV or movie screen. It remains clear once the movie ends and you look at the screen. Once your mental movie subsides, you are pure, free, and forever. Once this knowledge dawns, you can do anything you like and enjoy or suffer, but when you get caught up in your mind or misery, you know what or who is being affected. You can drive the car of your body but remain free.

Only the body and mind can suffer, as the true Self is eternally free and never can change. The True Self, You, forever are, even when you forget and begin to suffer. That which remains is always unborn, undying and unchanging, pure, free, and forever. Since this truth is indescribable and unknowable by the mind, you must have a direct experience or awakening, so this is the purpose of this expression I put into this book format.

We have spent so much time confirming ourselves as a body with a name and a mind with our thoughts, beliefs, and personality. Therefore, we never have to be concerned that we will not be able to use it as we like, but at the same time, allow it to be one with the fullness that we forever are. Unless you dissolve into the ocean of Pure Consciousness you will always be seasick! Keep reading about the true Self, meditating on it, and practicing, and you will know first-hand that freedom alone is!

What is Knowingness Meditation?

Transformation Meditation, also known as Know-ingness Meditation, is adapted from the direct teachings of Swami Shyam and the system of yogic meditation described in *The Yoga Sutras of Patan-jali.* It is based on observing or focusing on the space of Pure Consciousness, or the Knower of all experiences. You can utilize the ancient Sanskrit mantra, which is the guru mantra, *Amaram Hum Madhuram Hum,* or the English; I am immortal, I am blissful, or any other mantra that you choose. Your breath or the source of your breath can also be focused on as a starting point.

This system includes all the aspects of other mantra meditation techniques and the observing methods of Mindfulness Meditation, with the added aware-ness of the Pure Knowingness, or space that exists at the source, behind all the thoughts and tech-niques. It suggests that you de-identify with the changing thoughts in your mind and bring attention to the Knower, who is the experiencer or watcher of all the thoughts and forms. Through this de-identi-fication process, you can experience the peace and joy that is your true nature: pure, free, and forever.

Many beginning meditators think they can't medi-tate because they have too many thoughts or can't concentrate enough. This is the human condition, so most people have this idea. If you can't meditate, then no one can meditate, as everyone has thoughts and difficulty concentrating at times. This system of meditation does not require you not to have these challenges. It just suggests that you add this awareness with any of the techniques and accept that the human mind is that way, and it is not at all a hindrance to meditation.

Knowingness Meditation helps you understand the purpose, experience, and outcome of meditation physiologically, psychologically, and spiritually. This more complete knowledge of meditation will expedite the process by allowing you to understand what is happening in your mind, body, and nervous system while practicing meditation. This will enable you to be free from doubts about whether you are meditating correctly and to experience meditative awareness at any time. Meditative awareness is the direct knowledge of your true Self as pure, free, and forever!

From Mindfulness to Knowingness Meditation

Mindfulness Meditation has become a widely used method of meditation. It is remarkable that so many people are valuing and practicing meditation in schools, health centers, yoga classes, etc. Meditation is the best method to bring about a state of ease, relaxation, peace, joy, happiness, and fulfillment in one's life. The first step, which is to be mindful, is very important because, with most people, their attention is moving outward through the senses towards all the things and forms to find fulfillment in life. Many people are not mindful of their attention, which is always focused on that which is transitory and changing and can only bring temporary peace and satisfaction.

This first step of meditation practice, according to the Yoga Sutras of Patanjali, is called *pratyahar*, the inner turning of attention. Rather than turning your attention outward to all the experiences and things, you turn your attention inward by closing your eyes and observing or being mindful. Being mindful will also show you that there is you, the knower of the mind. This is the next step towards improved success in meditation. The key to remaining peaceful and happy in your life is the very sense of your Pure Knowingness. Knowing that you are the watcher, you are the knower of your mind and thinking, and then turning your attention to the Knower.

Right now, when you close your eyes, you can become aware that there is a space or screen in front of your closed eyes. This screen may appear dark or to have some color or light in it. Just like watching a movie or television screen, you can watch the screen of your awareness. Even when there are pictures on the movie screen, the pure screen is always behind the pictures even when you don't see them. In the same way, the pure screen of your consciousness is always at the back of your thinking. When you close your eyes you can know it, as you are the one who is knowing. Thoughts may come, may go, or stay on that screen. Some thoughts are helpful or useful, and some are upsetting and create uneasiness, but you can be mindful and just watch them. You can watch them come, watch them go, and watch when they stay. You can also notice when you react to them, when you become identified with them, and when you treat them as real and vital. Some thoughts are necessary and constructive, but others are destructive and cause fear, worry, doubt, pain, and suffering.

Knowingness is the key to your meditation because you come to know the Knower through your knowingness. As soon as you know the Knower you can become aware that the Knower is unchanging. Your Knower is always there, just like the screen behind the movie. The thoughts change, the feelings change, the mind changes, the body changes, the situations change, and life changes as the body ages. You change every day from the waking state to the sleep state, to the deep sleep state, to the dream state, and then back to the waking state.

All these states of consciousness are changing but you, the Knowingness state, or the transparent screen is what never changes. So now we are making a noticeable shift to pay attention to the one who knows, through your Pure Knowingness.

This technique can be practiced through a few different methods. Watching the breath going in and out and or watching the pauses between each breath, after the inhalation before the exhalation, and after the exhalation before the next inhalation. These are some methods because in that pause or space, you, the Knower, remain. There is no identification with any thought or feeling in that pause. It's just you, Pure. We are moving the attention toward purity, towards Knowingness, or the true Self or being that you are.

If you prefer, you can use the mantra, as it can make it easier to meditate. As you may often be caught in your thinking, a mantra helps by bringing in only one thought to focus on. *Ma* means mind, and *tra* means to release. Repeating a mantra releases you from all the various thoughts that are going through your mind. If there is the thought, "I didn't do that right," you feel bad. If there is a thought, "I excelled at that," you feel good. You have become identified with your thinking.

To become free from your thinking or de-identified, you can know yourself as the watcher or the knower of the thinking. Thoughts often come without your invitation, so you cannot stop them from coming. Instead, you can know yourself as the knower of your thinking. When a thought comes, "I did not do that right," you can act on it if you like; you can change what you did wrong, but you are not worried about it; you are not involved with it. You now know that right and wrong are not your qualities, the very Knowingness.

The Knowingness that you are is always free from right or wrong, good or bad. Then, your decisions come from Pure Knowingness and not from the limited experiences within your mind. Through this mastery, by coming to know the Knower, you still function in the same way, doing everything good to do. You can fulfill any desires you wish but, are not bound by whether they are completed or not. You know that you already are that peace, love, and joy that is unchanging as you are the Knower and your mind, your feelings, or your thinking do not limit you.

The mantra given to me by my Swami-ji is *amaram hum madhuram hum*. The meaning is that I am pure, free, and forever the immortal blissful Knower. *Amaram hum madhuram hum*. You can repeat it silently to yourself, *amaram hum, madhuram hum, amaram hum, madhuram hum*. If you forget the words or it becomes too tiring, you can just repeat *am hum*. Or you can use any mantra that you prefer.

The purpose of the mantra is to keep your attention on one thought, a peaceful thought, rather than many agitating thoughts that can go through your mind. Those thoughts, however, may still come, but it's okay. No problem to the meditator if thoughts come because you can keep repeating a higher thought, *amaram hum, madhuram hum*. But again, the key to this meditation is to know the Knower who can repeat *amaram hum madhuram hum*, who is repeating *amaram hum madhuram hum*.[1]

That Knower is You pure, free, and forever. You can practice after reading this or listen to one of my audios[2] to know how to pronounce it correctly. Then

---

[1] Please see Shree's website for the links to her podcasts and meditation app audios. [1] www.transformationmeditation.com

use it whenever you like to keep knowing the Knower, *amaram hum madhuram hum, amaram hum madhuram hum.* Pure, free, and forever, you are!

Doubt Free Meditation in Five Minutes

When so many wonderful benefits have been attributed to the practice of meditation why doesn't everyone meditate? Why is it so difficult for most people to sit quietly by themselves for a few minutes in meditation? Since the nature of the waking state human being is activity, to sit quietly when the mind is active rather than to take up an action to fulfill one's daily chores or future desires, goes against the waking state's functioning of the mind. The human mind is a never-ending loop of thoughts such as: joy, happiness, fear, worry, concern, agitation, the desire for more happiness and the avoidance of unhappiness. Whatever the most dominant event, current or past, that is remembered in one's thought it begins to dominate one's mind. This rounding of thoughts continues even without your suggestion or encouragement.

The mind functions to move toward achieving and engaging in activities to bring about happiness and avoid unhappiness. To sit at rest, unless you are exhausted or tired, goes against what the mind wants. You want to just keep thinking, with the belief that eventually you will figure out what to do to make something change and get what you think you need or want from it. The belief is that you will finally be satisfied when you get your desire fulfilled and then you can rest. But this satisfaction or happiness only occurs temporarily when the desire gets fulfilled until it changes, or the next desire comes. This endless wheel of thoughts, feelings, desires, and actions keeps turning and turning, until one day the last breath is taken and that is called death or the end of life.

When one becomes aware that the mind, thoughts, and experiences of life are sometimes wonderful and other times painful then one starts to wonder if there is another way to experience satisfaction that is not dependent on change. When one knows that the nature of the human being is sometimes health and other times sickness, sometimes happy and other times miserable, sad, or disappointed; one begins to look for other ways of experiencing life whereby one does not have to suffer. You become aware that even when you experience happiness, maybe at the start of a new relationship or marriage or in making a lot of money, there is inherent unhappiness—the fear that this happiness can be lost one day. Therefore, if happiness and unhappiness, apparent opposites, seem to appear together, are they made of the same thing? When you get fed-up trying to find permanent joy, peace and health through the changing body, mind and situations in your life, you are ready to begin the practice of meditation.

Meditation is the most essential practice for true freedom from the waking state mind, through unfolding a state of highest awareness. The mind must be purified through meditation practice for it to not keep functioning with attachment and fear, which is present only on the level of the mind. You can understand the workings of the mind and stop believing in it as the ultimate truth. The truth of the mind is changing, and the truth of the Self is unchanging. So now begin to meditate, purify the mind and transform the changing waking state of consciousness—the state of mind based on pleasure and pain, happiness and unhappiness—into the Fourth State, the meditative awareness that is forever unchanging.

The mind must become absorbed in the Self, it's very source, for you to live in the unchanging bliss of the Self. You have always been this source or Self, but it gets covered, like the clouds cover the sun even though it is always there in the sky. Through the practice of meditation, you will function most perfectly in your everyday life and accomplish all that you desire even more efficiently and productively then before, but you will remain free from the destructive power of the changing mind and its thoughts. When a useful thought comes you can act on it. When a destructive thought comes you can watch it and let it go by not believing or entertaining it more than is necessary.

It is essential to know how your meditation practice can be most effective, so you'll have no doubt about the methods that you are applying. It may seem difficult to achieve as meditation is a state of highest awareness and not a state of the mind. Since you are usually so focused on thoughts, concepts, and ideas, you will doubt if you are meditating correctly and effectively when the mind still has thoughts and concerns. Even after meditating for many years, you may not know how well you are progressing or if you are benefiting the most from your practice.

Here is what will work. First you apply one of the many techniques of meditation. Then your only job is to be with yourself, however you are. You sit and watch and whatever happens—thoughts, no thoughts, images, no images, colors, no colors, etc.––you just be. You are not doing, trying to create something, or trying to make something happen, or even just taking yourself too seriously. You are watching, and accepting it all, whatever is going on or not going on. This way you tune-in directly to the meditative awareness which is always present. You can't try to find it, or make it happen. It never left you. It is the canvas behind everything else. Like when you see the TV screen you know that the light gets projected onto it and appears as if the screen has turned into the many images. In the same way, you never changed or became anything other than the clear screen space. Your thoughts and images are just projections. So, your only job is to be that Pure Space that is unchanging. Be the one who you have always been.

Through this freedom in your practice, you start to really enjoy the bliss of Being. Not trying to change anything but just being with You. You come to see that your true nature is blissful just like you are in deep sleep when nothing is bothering you. You then, naturally want to meditate more often as you enjoy it so much. Why wouldn't you want to do what you enjoy?

You can set up a conducive environment by first practicing breathing techniques or chanting to settle your active mind and body, then read something inspirational on this knowledge or listen to one of our recordings of a talk about higher awareness and then you close your eyes and be. That Being is the Knower, and only when you know the Knower are you in the doubtless state. Until you know the Knower, doubt must remain. Until then you just have faith and trust that if you can be free from all doubt every night in deep sleep, then you can also be doubt-free while awake. This freedom from all doubt unfolds when you watch the space of your

Pure Being and know yourself as the Knower, forever pure and free!

Am I Meditating Effectively?

How Can you Get the Maximum Benefit from your Meditation Practice?

The question: "Am I meditating effectively and getting the maximum benefit from my meditation?" is often asked by those beginning meditation, but more advanced meditators also ask it. When someone asks if they are walking correctly, an expert can watch and see how the legs and hips move and give them the answer. Meditation, however, is focused on that which is formless, and it is done inside, so therefore, no one can watch you and answer this question by observing you. As you meditate with closed eyes and watch the inner spaces that are formless, you can easily get confused about what you are supposed to be watching and what is supposed to be happening in your meditation. You may then question if you are meditating correctly or at all and if you are getting the most results from your practice.

For a human being, most tasks are accomplished while working with objects, persons, or thoughts, and by doing the task effectively, you achieve the desired result. In meditation, you are practicing non-doership. You are observing the one who knows the objects, body, and thoughts, and you are observing the space in front of your closed eyes—the inner silence. From the perspective of non-doership, the inner watchfulness is opened through what is called *pratyaahaar* in Patanjali's system of

AshtangYog or The Eight Limbs of Yoga, and then you move into what is called *dhaarana*, cultivating the power of attentiveness and then the seventh limb or *dhyaan*, meditation. Meditation allows the attention to flow toward the source, and it culminates in *samaadhi*, the eighth limb, which is the complete evenness of the intellect or the Vision of Oneness.

If you are not experiencing more ease and peace in your life, it is because you are never leaving the waking state except for when you go to sleep. This is not your fault, as the very human condition is to live in just three states of consciousness: waking, dreaming, and deep sleep. When you begin to turn your attention to the Knower of these three states, through your meditation practice, you begin to open to the fourth state or meditate state. If this has still not unfolded, then more practice is essential for it to unfold.

If you take up the practice of *Ashtang Yog* or the Eight limbs of Yoga, you will systematically move into the meditative state by first purifying the body and mind, cultivating easiness in your body through *hatha yoga* exercises, purifying the nerve channels through *praanaayaam* or the regulation of your breath.

Through this practice, your mind will become still, and you will more easily be able to bring attention to the source of your thoughts. Then you can discriminate between what is changing mind and what is the unchanging Self. Through this practice of *vivayk khyati*, or perfect discrimination, you will experience your own peace forever shining inside. Meditation and perfect discrimination allow one's attention to flow toward the source and culminate in *samaadhi*, the complete evenness of the intellect—the Vision of Oneness!

When the attention moves inward and leaves the gross sense level, you realize that your enjoyment is not coming completely through sensual experiences. You turn your attention to the source of your thoughts and feelings and come to know the source of your Being. You begin to live in the fourth state of consciousness. If you have difficulty doing this in silence, then listening to an audio recording will help lead your attention to the meditative space. This will allow you to meditate more easily and get the benefits of the fourth state of consciousness.

Established in the fourth state, communicate more effectively with others because you become more compassionate, seeing everyone as your own Self, the space that you now know through meditation. You can accept whatever is happening in your life that is beyond your control. You no longer rely solely on worldly experiences for your satisfaction and happiness; you have a well of happiness inside that you are now tuned into. That eternal well that is completely fulfilling and satisfying you. And you can act with ease and overcome all obstacles in life.

Continue your meditation practice and keep knowing yourself as the Knower. The more you are in touch with You, the Knower, the more you can transform your waking state and live in the fourth state, living your life free from the pain and suffering that is experienced in the waking state. Through Transformation Meditation practice and teaching and sharing this with others, you will transform the waking state and live in the Vision of Oneness filled with joy and peace.

Teaching Mindfulness and Knowingness from the Himalayan Masters

Meditation is now on the lips and minds of every intelligent person. The scientific results show that everyone can greatly benefit from meditation for improved health, peacefulness, relaxation, better sleep, and happiness. Meditation is taught to school children, university students, corporate executives, politicians, health care professionals, exercise, yoga teachers, and seniors who want to enjoy their golden years in peacefulness and harmony.

Where do you start if you want to develop your meditation practice so that you are fully established in meditative awareness and feel confident enough to teach meditation? You can become a meditation teacher, life coach, or even just share meditation with those you love. The United Nations declared December 21st as the International Meditation Day.

Transformation Meditation provides direct, personal knowledge and experience of the space of the highest meditation that usually hides within. You can teach Mindfulness Meditation as you would teach or facilitate any other subject, but with this added direct, personal knowledge and experience that Transformation Meditation provides, you will be living meditation. This direct experience will enable you to be a much more effective and appreciated meditation teacher.

You will quickly move from Mindfulness Meditation to Knowingness through Transformation Meditation. This practice will lead you from the awareness of the present moment, filled with thoughts, images, and sounds, to the direction of the Knower, or the one who is watching and knowing all the thoughts, physical sensations, and experiences. From the direct perception of the Knower, you will never doubt you know the Knower. This Knowingness will now always shine within you, and all those who come in your presence will want to know how to have your great sense of peacefulness and bliss. Now, through these teachings and this direct connection with the state of peace, calmness, and blissfulness as it unfolds in you, teaching will become easy as you live in the very meditative state of highest awareness.

When you teach meditation and speak about meditation to your friends and family members, you also open your meditative awareness. This higher awareness enables you to live peacefully with ease and freedom. The best thing that you can do for yourself is to meditate and speak about meditation as much as possible. The best thing you can do for the world is to become established in the peaceful awareness of meditation and talk about it to others.

Peace begins with you! A peaceful person emanates a state of peace wherever they go. And, as you practice meditation, you'll radiate this vibration of peace so much that others will naturally want to know what you are doing. You can talk about meditation and lead them into meditation, and, again, this continues to support your practice, too. You will improve, your family members will improve, and the world will improve. Teach meditation and know the peace that you are: all is as One blissful Self.

The system of Transformation Meditation or Knowingness Meditation includes all the aspects of other mantra meditation techniques and the observing methods of Mindfulness Meditation, with the added awareness of the Pure Knowingness or space that exists at the source behind all the thoughts and techniques. It suggests that you de-identify with the changing thoughts in the mind and bring attention to the Knower. The Knower is the one experiencing or watching all the thoughts and forms. Through this de-identification process, you can experience the peace and joy that are part of your true nature. Instead of only identifying with the mind, you also identify with your true Self that is pure, free, and forever.

Laypeople, healthcare professionals, and yoga instructors practice Transformation Meditation and teach meditation to clients and students. It's not required that you receive a secret mantra, keep any secrets, or join any organization. Our methods are easily integrated into your everyday life. Transformation Meditation also helps you understand the purpose, experience, and outcome of meditation: physiologically, psychologically, and spiritually. Having this knowledge of meditation will expedite the process, allowing you to have a complete understanding of what is happening in your own mind, body, and nervous system. You'll be free from doubt and able to experience the meditative awareness at any time—the direct knowledge of your true Self—pure, free, and forever!

The Truth about Meditation and Samaadhi

What are the Common Misconceptions?

When we discuss what meditation is and is not, we can start by defining "meditate." Webster defines meditation as "to think deeply or focus one's mind for some time, in silence or with the aid of chanting, for religious or spiritual purposes or as a method of relaxation."

This definition is a start, but one needs to know more to practice it. Also, with just this information, many misconceptions about meditation can arise. Therefore, my working definition will be: "Meditation is a state of higher awareness, awareness of your true Self, which is pure, free and forever." If we use Webster's definition, meditation is only a focusing technique. However, the state of meditative awareness can occur spontaneously, such as, by being in the company of a long-time meditator, by listening to a talk on meditation, or just by closing your eyes and watching. Therefore, we need to expand the definition to do this. First, we will explore what meditation is not.

Misconception 1: The state of yoga or union with the Self is achieved when the thoughts in the mind are controlled.

Thoughts do not need to be controlled. Your mind is a field of thoughts, and they appear without your

23

invitation. When you come to know that your thoughts are waves of perception that you, as the Self, use to perceive the world, then your thoughts are not problems that have to be controlled. They appear from the Source or Pure Consciousness, and you can observe them as they return to that same Source. When you follow these thoughts back to the Source or experience the space between your thoughts, you are united with the Self. When ice is heated, it turns to water and then steam, which dis-solves back into space. H20 can appear in different forms, such as clouds, ocean waves, foam, ice, steam, etc., but it is the same substance. In the same way, your thoughts can be seen as changing energy or in a more solid form as words. They are waves of perception that you can observe and watch as they dissolve back into the Pure Consciousness or the background field of your awareness. In the same way that we know that the ocean is all water, even though we may perceive waves, spray, or foam, we can know that thoughts are all Pure Conscious-ness.

Misconception 2: Meditation is a technique that you must practice daily to obtain results.

There are numerous techniques and practices that can be used by those who want to learn how to med-itate. Meditation is a state of higher consciousness or awareness. When you are in the meditative awareness or the direct experience of the fourth, or meditative, state of consciousness, the job is done. At that time, a technique was not needed. Therefore, the technique or theory of meditation is only needed by those who do not have direct experience. Once the direct experience unfolds and continues, you are always in meditation.

Meditation, or the fourth state of consciousness, the *samaadhi* state, permeates all the other states, such as waking, deep sleep, and the dream state. Just like you wake up from a dream and know that the dream is not the reality, in the same way, you wake up from the waking state and know that the waking state is not the reality. The fourth state, also called the knowingness state, higher awareness, or the awakened state, is always your reality. Therefore, it is when you forget this awareness, or it becomes covered by the waking state mind and thoughts, that you need a technique to remind the mind of its originality or space that remains when the waking state dissolves into its source.

Misconception 3 – Meditation will make you healthy.

Meditation is a practice and lifestyle that will free you from the rigid fixity of believing yourself as only a physical body and mind. Most people are limited to this physical perception. When you know the meditative awareness, space, or pure Knower as who you are, then there is never any disease. Illness and disease only come to the body and mind of a human being. So, for you, the pure Self, there is never any disease. This does not mean that the body is not subject to illness or pain.

The body, like any vehicle such as your car, will have its issues and challenges. You can buy a new car, and it runs for many years without any problems, or it can have many mechanical issues and even be called a "lemon." You take care of your car as much as possible and give it the necessary checkup and servicing, and you do the same for your body, but there is never a guarantee that it will not break down. There is no definite cause and effect. Just like your mother can do all she can do to have a healthy pregnancy, but she is not in total control of the birth and the health of her baby. We can only do our best, and the rest is up to the nature of the universe or what can be called God. God, or the universal being, in the yogic perspective, is the Pure Consciousness that is the very life of all.

The human body can have cancer as a young baby or, at birth, have a faulty heart. Others are born without any major health concerns but have them at an older age. It is not under the power of human beings that the body has or doesn't have these issues, just like it is not your fault that the car is a lemon. The body needs to function according to its laws and system, so there is only so much you can do to delay these inevitable happenings. Call it genetics or lifestyle; it doesn't matter. Both come into play.

You can live a totally healthy life with a good vegetarian or plant-based diet, have good company, and meditate every day and still have a stroke or get cancer. This doesn't mean that you have no control at all. All your healthful practices may allow you to live in a state free from worry and anxiety and in as much ease and health as possible. But there is no physical immortality or total health of the body. When you think in this way, such as in some new age teachings, you can feel bad as if you have caused your own illness through your negative thinking or habits. Instead, you can know that for you, the Self, there is no illness because you are not your limited changing body form that dies.

The body will need to have some pretext to dissolve back into its originality. Whether this happens before birth, at birth, or at one hundred-plus years, it is not your true concern. Living a *sattwic*, or balanced, lifestyle will benefit you by allowing you to live each moment in meditative, blissful, free awareness. Then, even when your body is sick or hurt, you know that You, the Pure Self, are never sick or hurt! Just like your car can be stalled or totaled, you remain untouched. The body car can have issues, but not you, the Pure Being.

This knowledge allows you to live as healthy as possible in your body without the fear and worry that it will break down and without blaming yourself for not being perfect in your lifestyle choices. Everyone's body will eventually break down. With the knowledge that You, the Pure Being, never dies, you are free from this limited form and any blame of yourself and others. Whether the body dissolves back into the earth earlier or later is not of concern to the Realized One. You only preserve the body for your liberation and realization so you can feel easy and remain in meditation.

Misconception 4-You must give up your physical and material desires, relationships, worldly attachments, and live simply.

Swami-ji would often say that you don't have to give up anything, just add meditation, and that you don't get freedom through bondage. These are very important statements, as without meditation, it may be impossible for you to give anything up. Why would you want to give something up that you think is your source of satisfaction? When you begin to meditate, you get a revived energy or power in your system, and you no longer want to do the things that don't fully serve your body's health and well-being. You don't give up your freedom. You change your view of what true freedom is.

You can live in a significant relationship or alone, but either way, you know that your true freedom is not bound by being with anyone or by being alone. You remain aware of the contentment and satisfaction that you already are, so the things that you desire, or need are not your limited focus. You still work towards your goals, but you are not dependent on achievement to bring about your happiness, fulfillment, or satisfaction in life. You are completely self-contained and free and simultaneously have a wealth of love and affection to share with your family, friends, and loved ones. You have unbound energy to complete all your projects and live life most fully.

This we observed daily by watching Swami-ji. He wrote and published at least fifty books, numerous writings, and thousands of poems, and spoke every day in satsang. He also met with people in small groups before or after the two-to-three-hour satsang. He also built and landscaped an ashram with many buildings and homes. He did not sleep or rest that much as it was not needed, and he always moved with total freedom and delight. It never appeared that he was working too hard, and yet he accomplished more than most people could think was humanly possible.

Now that we have delineated the misconceptions on the path of meditation, we can continue with the discussion of the truth about meditation. The question will arise: "If you do not control your thoughts in meditation, then what do you do?" The answer is that you just close your eyes and watch the space in front of your closed eyes. The instruction is to watch the space and the thoughts as they are. In this watching, you become aware that you are the watcher or witness of all the changing thoughts. Therefore, you can de-identify with the thoughts and remain the Knower of your thoughts. You become aware that you are not your thoughts, as you are the one who is knowing or watching your thoughts.

The techniques of meditation that include using a mantra or watching the breathing are just preliminary methods to allow you to begin to watch rather than drift off with all the changing thoughts. When you follow all your thoughts, that is called daydreaming, not meditation. It becomes meditation when you are the watcher or Knower of your mind and thoughts. When you direct your attention back to the mantra that you are repeating, or when you direct your attention to watching your breath. By doing this, you are remaining the watcher or Knower and de-identifying with the changing thoughts. You become aware that you are the watcher or subject, and the thoughts are what you are watching or knowing as the object.

If you, for some time, follow the thoughts, then that is fine, as you cannot control your mind. Thoughts just come from nowhere; as your hair grows without your control, so your thoughts come and go without your control. When you go to sleep at night, you lie down on your bed, tuck yourself in, and wait for sleep to come. In the same way, when you meditate, you close your eyes, watch the space in front of your closed eyes, repeat the mantra, or watch the breath, and become aware of the Knower of the thoughts and your breath, and then meditation occurs by it-self. Meditation is "A state or higher awareness, not the technique that gets you to that knowingness."

Patanjali in his great work on the yoga sutras, says in his
Yog Darshan these truths.[3]

III:2: *Tatra pratyya-aikataanataa dhyaanam*
Dhyaan, or meditation, occurs when the attention of the mind flows in conscious continuity and opens to the awareness of its own knowingness[1].

To remain aware of your own knowingness means to remember the Knower. The space behind your thoughts, or the space when all the thoughts dissolve back into that space, is what remains when you allow your thoughts to just pass by. You remain as You, the Knower, or Pure Knowingness, and that You is pure, free, and forever. That is meditation!

Samaadhi is not the type of transcendence whereby you no longer exist, and you are unconscious, as it often sounds like when it is described as transcendence. *Samaadhi* is when the *buddhi* (*dhi*), or intellect, is *sam*, or even.

III:3-*Tad-ayv-aarth-maatra-nirbhaasam-swaroop-shoonyam-iv samaadhi*

In that same *dhyaan,* or meditation, when only the essential purity of the focus of meditation shines in the meditator's mind as if the mind's dualistic

---

[3] From *The Sootras of Patanjali Yog Darshan: Concise Rendition,* by Robert William Eaton.

nature has dissolved and become absorbed into the pure space of the Self. That is *samaadhi*, the state of indivisibility or oneness in the meditator.

When in the state of *samaadhi* there is no longer the dualistic vision of you as a Knower and a space that is being known. There is only You, the Knower, or the purity of space. When the intellect is absorbed back into the space from where it arose, just like clouds dissolve into the blue sky, and now there are no clouds, in the same way, the wave of perception or thought is dissolved into You, the pure Knower-space or Pure Knowingness itself.

Samaadhi is the Eternal Being. In *samaadhi*, there is no desire or craving for anything as you are completely fulfilled and free just by being left alone with your true Self. Nothing else is needed, and acquiring everything else is possible. All the clouds of mental thoughts, feelings, and forms have now dissolved back into the Source or clear space. That space is now You, the Pure Knowingness, and all is peaceful and free. *Samaadhi* is your true state or true nature, as it is always behind all your thoughts and experiences. The space of your purity gets covered by the mind; therefore, when the mind is absorbed in that space, what remains is the true You, pure, free, and forever.

Eight Steps to Self-Realization

1. Know the Peace that you have in deep sleep. Peace is unchanging; your mind is changing.
2. Know the Knower of your mind.
3. Meditate on the Knower, not on the mind.
4. Be Aware of the distinction between the mind and the Self: division and Oneness.
5. Choose the Self or Peace and not the mind.
6. Trust in the Self as the solution and not in the mind.
7. Create a *Sattwic* lightness in the mind and body through yoga, *praanaayaam,* and a yogic diet.
8. Know that You are forever, Before birth and after death.

If you are like me, or most people who journey onto the path of Self-Realization, you want to know how to be free from the problems and difficulties that you find as a human being on earth. If you have experienced meditative awareness or have an epiphany regarding your true essence and the Oneness of all, you want to know how to maintain that direct experience.

Maybe you have already studied many different psychologies, spiritual theories, methods, and techniques. Now, you want to find the most efficacious and clear way to realize that which is the truth of your own Being, to fulfill the purpose of your life. There are so many books, scriptures, masters, teachers, disciplines, hypotheses, and systems of enlightenment that you may feel overwhelmed with information and ideas. Everyone seeks a clear-cut, easy-to-follow system that takes the minimum amount of time and effort and brings about the maximum results.

We all want to experience freedom from pain, fear, agitation, anxiety, worry, and doubt. To be relaxed, peaceful, loving, and easy, you must start from where you are: a human being with a body, a mind, senses, and all the conditions, concepts, and beliefs that have been developed from a lifetime of practice and repetition.

When you are born as a baby, before your mind develops and is filled with so many thoughts and conditions, you are naturally blissful. We all love to look at a newborn baby or little toddler. We see the pure bliss bubble that they are and the unobstructed light in their eyes. From this observation - of the bliss of a baby, we can see that as soon as the mind develops, problems begin, along with the thoughts in the mind.

Through our thinking process, we can now analyze how, in deep sleep, there are no problems, worries, or concerns. The problems on the level of the body and mind only arise in the waking state of consciousness. The human mind must develop so that you can interact and function in the world. However, this very development of the human mind can also limit our happiness and fulfillment in life unless the mind is purified through meditation and the highest knowledge.

As human beings, we are victims of the human condition, subject to the functioning of the body, mind, and senses. The body, being a bundle of nerves, hormones, blood, organs, bones, skin, and senses, has a physiological functioning that is often not in our direct, voluntary control. We must admit that we are not the sole doer. There is another force or power that is moving our body and mind, and from that unseen power, all the actions occur. You breathe and digest your food without your conscious control. You fall asleep without making it happen.

The knowledge in meditation gives you the solution to all human difficulties without us making it happen. All suffering has one and only one cause. And when you know that cause is ignorance of your true Self, then you can know the solution. When you have a direct experience of the fourth state of consciousness, the meditative awareness, you no longer need to do anything other than remain with it.

Through the study and practice of meditation, you become aware that if you start from the idea that you are a human being, limited to your body and mind, you will remain ignorant of the true Self. Then all the problems mentioned above will have to occur. Just like the eyes are made to see, the ears are made to hear, the human system is made to enjoy and to suffer; to experience pain and pleasure and to react to various stimuli to fulfill all the human desires.

First, you need food and shelter to take care of the physical system. When those physical desires are fulfilled, mental desires come about, experienced by a craving from the physiological system, so you can have more comfort, ease, and happiness for your mind and body. The human being keeps striving for more and more, bigger and better, as there is a sense of lack in the waking state with the unending desire to fulfill it. This mechanism is useful and productive. It keeps the species continuing through procreation, and then by society advancing, it

creates more technological, ecological, and eco-
nomic improvements.

This mechanism only becomes a detriment when it
is based on greed, jealousy, fear, and self-aggran-
dizement. Then, the mindset functions only to have
your individual needs and desires fulfilled. Then,
you may neglect and destroy the environment and
the lifestyle of others. Therefore, it is how one oper-
ates the mechanism that will lead to the highest vision with mutual support and appreciation of the
Whole.

We need to have a human system to function in this
world. The baby is born helpless but grows into
awareness and develops skills to function in the
world. The physical system is used, and the mind
begins to think about how to get what it needs and
wants. But you've discovered that this longing and
discomfort in the human system does not end just
by getting what you think you want by fulfilling your
desires. There is always more wanting and desiring
just around the corner. That is how the human system works. It is not your fault, and you cannot
change this functioning of the human system. But
there is a tried-and-true path for you to follow that
will lead you out of all human suffering.

The solution to this dilemma is not in the waking
state. If you are in the waking state, the system continues to act in the way that it was meant to function. Without higher awareness you can be completely identified as being that human system, with
a mind and body. If you remain tagged or rooted
only to your physical system, as only a human being, you will continue to enjoy and suffer. The solution, then, is not to remain only a human being but

to awaken to a higher state of consciousness by coming to know the true Self or Knower that you forever are. Since the cause of all suffering is ignorance of your true Self, then the solution is knowledge of your true Self. The only way to get all your desires fulfilled is to not have desires.

Since you must start from where you are, you accept that you have become a human being, and you are awake in the waking state. Then you can bring in the discrimination that you are the Knower of your mind and body and not limited to your thoughts and physiological suffering. Whenever the mind arises in the waking state, you need to have a method to bring your attention back to the Knower, to dissolve the mind into its source, which is forever free and blissful. This method is the practice of meditation, higher thinking, and Self-awareness to awaken you into higher consciousness.

In this state of highest awareness, you know the bliss of your true self is self-effulgent and not dependent on fulfilling your desires or on having any situation change. In any situation that you find yourself in, you can bring in this awareness and meditate on who you truly are. Your body continues to function, and your life continues as it is, but you can remain in a state free from all the agitation and worry that is inevitable when you are living only in the waking state of consciousness.

You don't have to expect anything more of the waking state than what it can provide but you know the way out. Most psychological therapies are limited as they are designed to make you feel more comfortable in the waking state or to reduce your stress, anxiety, or depressions. They do not allow you to experience and know your own free state of being which is self-effulgent and not dependent on anyone or anything else.

In psychology, this can be known as the transpersonal self, as it is beyond what you consider your personal reality. However, it is not only transpersonal as it is a state of Oneness with the Whole, so it includes everything. Knowing the Self, forever free that you are, is the solution state and answer to all your concerns and difficulties. This is the Vision of Oneness as you become aware of yourself as One with the Whole, which is like the sky or Pure Consciousness. You need to make this shift to know the Oneness, which is the true Knower and your true I. Then, all the solutions will come to you from this higher state of consciousness, which is the very solution state.

Again, if you are at all like me, or like most people, you find that there is just too much to do. So, adding anything more makes you feel defeated before you have even begun. That is why I developed the *Eight Steps to Self-Realization.*[4] You can apply these steps at any time during your day, regardless of what you are doing. They are strengthened when you take even a few moments in silent meditation or by just listening to a recording. But they are also applicable to use whenever your mind brings you to a state of pain or suffering. After some time of listening to them they become a part of you, as they are you. Then, it will become effortless to practice at any time, just like it is now effortless for you to know when someone calls your name, you know that it is

---

[4] Please see Shree's website http://www.transformedu.com for her books and the links to the apps with her audio meditations.

you. In the same way, you will come to know the Knower as your true nature–pure, free, and forever.

Know the Blissful Knower
Through Meditation

All intelligent people now know that meditation dramatically benefits those who practice it. Even so, few people practice regularly to gain the incredible benefits. Why? Those who have not learned meditation correctly may find it hard to adopt a new behavior, even though they know it will benefit them. Lifestyle patterns are fixed and can't easily break without proper guidance, inspiration, and structure. Many people have tried to learn meditation by listening to an audio recording, reading an introductory description, or reading the meditation technique, which has left them in a quandary about how to practice correctly. They may ask: "What am I supposed to experience? Am I doing it the right way? My mind keeps thinking thoughts, and I can't stop them?"

A great deal of information regarding meditation is incomplete or confusing. Many people, after unsuccessful attempts, think they cannot meditate. Since their minds are busy with active thoughts, they conclude they cannot become peaceful or free from thinking. Their lifestyle and schedules are just too hectic!

Also, meditation philosophy is often associated with religious, ritualistic, or monastic practices that can be impractical, uncomfortable, cultish, or confusing to the average person. Most people want to learn to relax and become peaceful. The deeper aspects and understanding of meditation—although obtusely delineated in ancient scriptures—can be challenging to comprehend and assimilate into a modern lifestyle without direct and sustained instruction from a seasoned meditation teacher.

The basic techniques of meditation are fundamentally straightforward. They are often listed in magazines or on social media. But practicing these simple techniques without adept knowledge is like trying to cook a recipe with a list of ingredients but no step-by-step directions. The list of ingredients alone is not enough information to help you make a delicious meal. Likewise, reading about what constitutes a meditation technique—the essential ingredients—may inspire you to try but, ultimately, lacks the step-by-step guidance and encouragement to sustain and mature your practice.

Meditation is often taught only as a technique for relaxation, as the meditative state cannot be known directly by the mind. Therefore, one cannot experience it thoroughly using a method only meant to quiet the mind. Peace cannot be found permanently on the level of the mind. The mind's job is to think and generate thoughts, so it cannot always remain peaceful. A higher mind must be unfolded through the purification of the lower mind. The Knower of the mind must be revealed to you in your meditation.

The mind of a human being has many functions and abilities, but it can also limit your ability to remain peaceful and free. When the mind is not engaged in thoughts and objects, the Pure Being that you are is always quiet. The Pure Being is unchanging; however, because of the nature of the mind, which covers your true Self, you cannot know the peace that is forever shining. To know this unchanging peace directly, you must experience the subtle aspect of the meditation technique. This subtlest practice is to directly know the true Being or Knower that you already are. This is found at the source of your mind, the true Self, forever peaceful. Whether you are attending to it or not, the Being you are is forever and does not change. Only the body, mind, and thoughts change.

When you are in deep sleep, you are not engaged in your mind and thoughts. You do not have any worries, concerns, fears, anxiety, physical pain, or suffering of any kind. From this, you can see that all the troubles come to you due to waking up and engaging your mind in your thinking. As soon as you wake up, you become I, an ego personality with a body and a mind. Then, all your superimposed conditions, beliefs, ideas, credentials, relations, and possessions reappear, just as they disappeared when you went to sleep the night before.

Through the practice of meditation, you can inquire into the true or unchanging I—the I, which is not only the mind and the body. The individual I is known in the waking state, the dreamer's I in the dream, and the nonexistent I in deep sleep. It is the Knower who knows that you have a mind and a body, that you were asleep, and that you were dreaming.

This Knower is the unchanging consciousness. It remains throughout whether you are awake, sleeping, or dreaming. When you know the Knower, which is the real or unchanging I, the true Being, you are in the meditative awareness, the Fourth State of Consciousness, or Higher Consciousness. It is the unchanging blissful state that you also experience every night in deep sleep, but when you are asleep, you cannot function, so you do not experience what is called the world. When you are awake, and the Pure Being or Knower knows the Knower, then you are in the Fourth State of Consciousness; this is meditation.

You can live in this Fourth State of Consciousness while you are awake. In this state, you use your mind and body as tools to experience the world, but you know that you are the Knower of your mind and thoughts. Then, the mind does not have power over you. You gain this mastery when the covering of your mind dissolves, and what remains is your true Self.

This practice of transformation in meditation will bring about all the results you want in terms of peace, happiness, joy, and freedom. You can live your life in the flow and current of the highest knowledge, which will guide you and allow you to remain established in peace and create whatever you need. The highest awareness is the only true freedom, as it is not dependent on health, wealth, or relationships.

The bliss of the Knower is self-effulgent. The Knower Self is one without a second, the Vision of Oneness. You can compare it to the sky, but it is vaster than the sky as it is all creative and unmanifest power. It is You. So, know the blissful Knower in your meditation, and this power will unfold as it has always been with you; it is You.

Imagine waking up in a shambled house with just one burner stove and barely enough clothes to wear, and you want to have more, but you cannot obtain it. You cry each day, wishing to enjoy a better life. You work hard in the field every day with chronic pain in your body, but you must continue to feed your family. Now imagine that you live in a mansion with everything that you need and more, but every morning when you wake up, you are worried about the stock market going down and all your relations and employees that depend on you for their livelihood. This lifestyle gives you constant strain and headaches. You fear not only for yourself but also to devastate so many others if you lose what you have.

Now, imagine if you knew that you were whole and complete as you are. If you never believed that you lacked anything or that you needed anything more. No matter what your bank balance is or whether you have a good job or inheritance coming your way, it doesn't trouble you. Inside your own Being, you know that you have everything you need and will need in the future. Imagine for a moment that you feel fulfilled and complete as you are.

You don't need anything outside yourself to fulfill your needs as you are entirely self-contained. You wake up in the morning, and your mind is absorbed in peace, and no worries, tensions, or fears touch you. That, whether you only have a roof over your head and a basic lifestyle with only a tiny one-burner stove and rice and beans to eat or if you live in a mansion with all the domestic help and amenities, you wake up established in a state of peace and freedom within your head. This peace is the genuine state in which everyone wants to live.

One method is to redirect your attention from the worried state by just taking a mental snapshot of it and letting it be stilled, then directing your attention to that peaceful state you have known in meditation and chose to live. The Sage Patanjali, the father of yoga philosophy, says that the only cause of human suffering is forgetfulness of your true Self. Therefore, if you are suffering in any way, rather than blaming it on yourself, others, or your life situations, you redirect your attention in meditation to your truth of being. Then you can be free of that suffering right now. The continued practices are just for you to maintain this awareness and not fall back into the human condition, which is some enjoyment and a lot of suffering.

As you know, you can imagine just about anything you choose with your imagination. Then why choose to imagine that you are lacking, that you are peaceless, and that you are an individual in a separate and scary world? Why not imagine that you are forever pure, free, and needless? To continually imagine that you are self-effulgent, free, and needless may seem difficult. Or, even if you can imagine this for a few minutes or days, your mind will come in and tell you that this is not true, and you will again think you are lacking and feel unfulfilled and worried.

To unfold a state of peace, fulfillment, and self-effulgence, no matter what your situation is as a human living in a separate world, you need a means to experience ease and freedom. You need to know how to unfold the state of highest consciousness that is self-effulgent and, therefore, self-sustaining. You need to understand how you can reach this state while living as a human being in the modern world. Thus, the practice of meditation and self-inquiry is essential.

The limbic or involuntary part of the brain is programmed to react to situations, and it is not directly in your control. If you see someone hurt on the road, you automatically go towards them to help them.

This behavior is a good life-supporting automatic re-action programmed into your brain. However, this same uncontrollable reaction in your brain is auto-matic when situations relate to past experiences where you had a bad experience. Then worries and fears are automatic, and you begin to suffer even though you can tell yourself it is not happening to you now. For instance, if you were once diagnosed with cancer and that created worry and fear, every time you go to a doctor, this automatic fear reaction occurs.

If you could, right now, know that the person you were in a deep sleep, where you had no bank bal-ance, worries, fears, concerns, or pain, is the same you. Then you could also wake up and no longer be-lieve that you are limited to your mind and thoughts and the automatic brain reactions that tell you that whatever you think is the truth. Such as, when you are feeling or thinking you are lacking or will have pain in the future, you believe that these thoughts are the truth, so you suffer. You don't want to suffer, but it unfolds automatically.

Most people would say that they do not on their own think they are pure, free, and forever, by just imag-ining or thinking this to be true. Therefore, a tech-nique or practice is essential, so we introduce the practice of meditation. By meditating on your own source, which is forever peaceful, you know the self-effulgent space that all is.

Through your repetition of the mantra (mind re-lease), your limbic brain reactions, based on past trauma or experiences, will be redirected. The med-itation will release the hold your brain has on you. Even when the physiological reactions may not change, you can know this is what is happening.

Then, you remain free from believing the thoughts and feelings that cause you pain.

The mantra is now only resounding in your head, *amaram hum madhuram hum,* I am pure, free, forever! You also stop believing in the thoughts and feelings that cause you happiness or pleasure when they are based only on the things that will change. Your body, mind, and emotions, as well as those of others, change, so the unchanging is the only trustworthy source of true and permanent peace.

From this true unchanging peace, you know this is the highest and only real prosperity. It is a state whereby you are self-contained and not troubled by the fears, worries, and doubts of the mind. From this, you come to know that the mind is illusory and your actual Being is the reality of all that there is. This Self-realized one will never feel a sense of lack as they remain tuned into the natural flow of the universe, which is entirely abundant and free. This Self-realized person will attract all they need and have a surplus of energy as their energy is not lost or wasted in worrying.

The abundance of life-supporting energy they now have can be shared with all who come in contact. Many people would want to be around this person and learn from them. They would know that this self-effulgent peace and ease was already there, so all else would be a bonus. Whatever is needed would come to them; others would want to help and support them so that they could learn from them and reach their ideal. Many would even want to give this person to be in their company and receive the teachings.

So now imagine the truth of who you are, totally content and free, and the true prosperity will be yours—as it is already You! This Self-realized person is You. You have always been that and will always be that. Through meditation, you will know who you already are at the source of your mind and your thoughts, and then this Self-effulgent Oneness, the highest and truest prosperity of all, will be known to you.

Knowingness Meditation: Enlightenment is Now

Knowingness meditation focuses on using the *sootras* of Patanjali and the Bhagavad Gita to realize the truth of these teachings right now. Not to have to study for a long time and practice endlessly, but for you to have the direct experience now. Then, your practice only maintains what you already know. These selected verses will give you the insight into how to help that unfold.

Patanjali Sootra 1:41. The unaware person believes in whatever thoughts appear in the mind. When they think of a positive thought, they are happy. When they think a fearful thought, they are worried. The Self/Being that is giving the very power to the mind has become forgotten because it is mixed or covered by the mind. The mind and senses become more substantial than the Self or Being.

With this mistaken perception, the intelligence, now only mental, is weakened. The mind appears firmer as the Self is covered from your awareness, so the Self seems weaker than the mind. Your deception is from the power of the Self, which has now become mixed with the mind, and now the mind thinks it is powerful. It is like if you plug a light bulb into an outlet, and you believe the bulb has the power. However, it would be just an unlit bulb without the electric current. The mind would be insentient matter without the Self or source of Pure Consciousness. As Swami-ji has said: "The mind thinks, and the Self realizes!"

As it says in the Bhagavad Gita III:42: The working senses are superior to dull matter; the mind is higher than the senses; intelligence is still higher than the mind; and he (the Self) is even higher than the intelligence. Without the Self shining its power, the intellect, mind, and sense would not function. (Bhagavad Gita commentary, Swami Shyam/Swami-ji).

Patanjali's *Sootra* I:41 makes us aware that the mind, compared to a crystal, takes on whatever color it reflects. When it remains the human mind, it takes on qualities such as doubt, fear, worry, happiness, and unhappiness. Through the transformation of the mind in meditation, the *vrittis,* or thoughts, are reduced or absorbed in the Self. The Self is the real power behind the mind, so now, the Self shines clearly without any coloration or doubts. It is like a clear crystal not clouded by imperfections, reflecting only its clarity and light. Your mind functions as a higher mind, and *vrittis,* or thoughts, do not bind you.

Patanjali Sootra I:42-47. Here we are given the discussion of the various stages of *samaadhi* (freedom from the mind). This knowledge is helpful when you begin meditation. You can start your focus on an object or thought and continue when the bliss unfolds until you know the "I alone." Through this practice, you observe how the true Self gets mixed with the thoughts in the waking state. You can then sift the true Self out of the mixture from the mind.

These initial stages of *samaadhi* are with the seed, or covering, as one can quickly revert to the waking state after practicing them. Just like if there is a

49

seed in the ground, it may sprout at any time. Even the blissful state in meditation is temporary, as it is not the ultimate state. There is still you, separate that is blissful. Also, in the "I am" state, your division of a separate I needs to dissolve into your Pure Self alone. Then it is called *asampragyaat samaadhi,* the highest attained state, Oneness alone. In this, one remains aware and free even while acting in the worldly dramas.

As Swami-ji has suggested, we need to experience *samaadhi* directly, as then, even if we lose it and revert into the other lower levels of the waking state, we will have faith that it will return. Then, due to our direct experience of *samaadhi,* we continue our practice as we begin to know that this highest attainment is already there. We are that *samaadhi,* so how can we ever be anything else?

You must contemplate these questions to know the ultimate answer. After hearing this knowledge, understand it right now! Continually seeking it will not work as you seek what is already present, so you keep missing it. It would be like if your eyeglasses are already on your head, but you search for them, as you can't see them, so you believe you have lost them. Remembering one's true nature, the Self-Aware Self, you reach the highest state of awareness through meditation. You remain in your essence, pure, free, and forever![5]

---

[5] To read more about this perspective of Patanjali's knowledge, see the book: *Knowingness Meditation: Enlightenment is Now,* by Sherrie (Shree) Wade. www.transformation-meditation.com

How to Overcome
Destructive Thinking

Beginning meditators often struggle with the idea that they want to meditate but cannot find the time or energy to do it. Most people are busy in life, making money and raising a family.

Meditators often think they have too many thoughts or are not practicing enough. Similarly, when you are on an exercise or weight loss program, you may think that even though you were compliant for a week, you slipped from your program afterward. Then, there can be self-degradation, frustration, and even giving up on the program.

Sage Patanjali makes it clear that the nature of the mind is to generate thoughts. Since the mind keeps generating thoughts, it is up to you as to which ones you believe and which ones you discard. You cannot stop the mind from thinking; that is its nature. But, if your thinking is destructive and not helpful, then you have the power to counteract those thoughts and not accept or believe in what the mind is telling you. When you think you haven't meditated enough, bring in the thought that even one meditation is of great benefit. Then, you can appreciate your success. When you overeat or eat unhealthy foods and think badly of yourself, cultivate the thought that, through awareness of your destructive thinking, you develop the power to change it. This awareness of yourself is, in and of itself, a positive achievement. First, there's awareness or mindfulness, then you develop the power to change your thoughts, and from that, you change your behavioral patterns.

Immediately after the discussion on the *yam*s and *niyam*s, purification techniques, Patanjali brings in a fundamental and valuable idea in Chapter II, Verses 33 and 34 - *Vitark abaandhanay pratipaksha bhaavanam*—when undesirable thoughts appear to encumber one's *saadhanaa* or yogic practice, one should cultivate desirable thoughts which will neutralize that negativity. To neutralize disturbing thoughts, one should cultivate *pratipaksha bhaavana*, the sense of reversing the focus of one's thinking or bringing in the opposite thought. Due to lust, greed, and attachment, one can develop a sense of mind that generates a quality of thinking based on destructive ideas.

If one has not developed himself in meditation practice, then the purification techniques given in the *yam*s and *niyam* are essential. If the person's mind is not yet purified, or free from lust, greed, and attachment, then they will be subject to this realm of thinking, and it will be challenging to practice the purification methods prescribed by Patanjali. Therefore, this verse is inserted right after the description of the injunctions and observances for purification and before the actual description for each method so you can know how to counteract any limiting thoughts in your mind that prevent you from doing your practice.

How can you be aware of your thinking? First, you must know that you are the Knower of your thoughts, not the victim. And you do not have to act on them unless you, the Knower, decide to. When the thoughts are of appreciation, and you make a positive change in your behavior, then reward and appreciate your efforts. This supportive encouragement of healthy living will generate more power to continue doing it. Rather than focusing on the times you neglect your meditation, exercise, or diet program and feel bad about it, reinforce your positive thoughts and behavior. Reading this is one of the positive steps in this evolution. Contemplation and practice will take you even further. You'll become aware that your ability to make changes is now unfolding from the infinite power generated in meditation.

It would be an endless process always to try and shape your thinking to be positive, so you also need another method to overcome destructive thinking. Negative thoughts are not dangerous or destructive unless you, the Self, identify with them and believe them to be true. They are a problem only when you give them energy and power. If you see them, instead, as waves of perception, you, the Knower, has the choice to act on them or just let them dissolve back into their source—the very ocean of Pure Consciousness. Just like a bubble in the sea dissolves and becomes the same ocean again. When you follow a thought back to its source, you become aware that it came from pure space or consciousness.

By remaining aware of yourself as the Knower of your thoughts, through meditation, you become aware of yourself as forever pure and not identified with your mind or its thinking. You purify your mind from its tendency to dwell on adverse reactions, and you gain the ability to master your mind, senses, and life.

Your habit patterns change effortlessly and quickly through meditation on the Knower. Then you have the direct experience of the Being, forever pure and free. Mastery of the mind is the result. These meditation techniques keep you focused on the Self, and you become aware that the Self, forever free, is who you are. You are no longer caught in your limited thinking, beliefs, or behaviors. You are the master free. Then, naturally, you do only those things that allow you to live your freedom and bliss.

Your appetite for overeating and eating the wrong foods changes. Your desire to not exercise and not take care of your health changes. And your ability to sit in meditation becomes more effortless. Now, you only enjoy those things that support your body and mind in living comfortably and healthfully so you can meditate and know the bliss forever residing inside.

Living in the Eternal Presence

I remember in college in 1974 when I first heard the slogan: "Be here now," I thought it was a revolutionary idea. I noticed that most of my thoughts were of the past. They were regrets or laments over what I could have done differently, what I wished would have happened, or what I hoped to change next time. I also considered the future, such as career desires, wealth, relationships, and possessions. These thoughts were based on removing my unhappiness or on getting the security, freedom, or ease that I craved to relieve my worry and anxiety. Because my thoughts were either about the past or the future, I could rarely enjoy what was happening before me or what I was doing in the present moment.

Although this "Be here now" concept was enlightening, I could not implement it. Even though I kept reminding myself: "Be here now!" I could not control my thoughts of the past and my aspirations for the future. Only in rare moments did I experience the "now." When eating something I enjoyed, out in nature, or spending intimate time with a friend, I could remain in the present moment of the here and now. Even when these present moment experiences were happening, I didn't examine what was really going on, so I was thinking of the here and now as another moment in time and space.

It wasn't until I learned the meditation technique that I could understand the true meaning of "here and now." Here and now is not in time and space but is the eternal presence. I could hear my teacher's words: "NOW, meditate!" In meditation, I noticed that I was the I, watching or knowing the thoughts and experiences that were either past, present, or future. That Knower was not involved in the thoughts or in time and space. I came to directly experience the bliss that is not on the level of the mind. It was the direct experience of the very life we are and that all this is here and now.

The life now became important, and I began to have a glimpse into the Me that is not bound by the intellect. The intellect can only grasp what is after appearance and before disappearance. Therefore, the intellect cannot know here and now. Here and now is that which is before birth, after death, and throughout the middle. Here and now is the unchanging bliss of the true Self. The intellect takes its power from that Pure Self or bliss and begins to say: "I am blissful." Then the, I assumes itself to be only the body and senses that is experiencing and not the Experiencer, or Knower.

When we examine from where the I arises and goes to, we will come to know the true I that is not caught in time in space. This I, is the very consciousness pure that never is born and never dies, so it is eternal. Then whatever is happening in the mind, whether thoughts of the past or future, or thoughts of the present experience, you remain the Knower of the mind or, the true Self, which is forever here and now. Then, the bliss of the Self is known to be the reality, and the changing forms are known also to be that same reality, which is Pure Space or Pure Consciousness.

Just as air can be still or begin to move as wind, the air is always air, so the Pure Consciousness or Self, can remain still or move into what we call thoughts or desires, but it is forever shining as here and now.

The Self is always filled with joy, health, life, and the knowledge of the unchanging here and now, that all this is,

The scriptures may imply that you must control your thoughts, renounce desires, and deny the ego. However, this is confused, difficult, or impossible. Therefore, those applying these methods have been unable to succeed. Trying to do this with the intellect won't work as the intellect cannot know the true Self or the "hear and now."

When you wake up in the morning there is the desire to become active. When you are in the waking state, you have many wants and needs, with some happiness and some unhappiness. If a higher state of consciousness is not known and directly experienced, then your life can only be based on trying to get the most happiness and reduce or remove the pain and suffering for yourself or others. Without knowledge of the Self, you and the world will remain fluctuating between happiness and unhappiness, and never feel easy, settled or free. Living in this freedom or the eternal presence is only possible when, in meditation, you directly experience your True Self, which is forever shining as the bliss of the eternal presence, which is always here and now.

When you live here and now in the eternal presence, the true Self is the reality. When that is known, what could there be more to desire, as you are already the Whole or Pure Space? What ego can there be to deny when you are already the infinite I, the bliss of the life itself? You are the purity, the freedom, the bliss of all that is.

Then the Seer, the Knower, remains established in its true nature." The Knower is who we are! So why wait to get it? Just know your True Self as the eternal presence, which is Pure, Free, and Forever right now[6]

---

[6] *Patanjali Yog Darshan* I:3, *"Tadaa drashtuh swaroopay'awasthaanam.*

Purifying The Happiness Nerve

As a mediator, one keenly observes how the mind and nervous system function. One observes that there is no happiness or unhappiness in a deep sleep, but as soon as one awakens, the conditions and concepts of the mind and body begin again. If the situations in one's life are positive, such as one's health, mood, family, etc., one may wake up happy. If the situations or conditions in one's life are not pleasing or difficult, one may wake up unhappy or miserable. In deep sleep, one is rested and peaceful. As soon as the mind arises in the waking state, when the same consciousness resting in deep sleep begins to identify itself as I and says, "I woke up," then the problems can begin.

So much information is available these days regarding the necessity of proper diet and exercise to live a healthy and happy life. Although these health rules are fundamental to observe to live a longer and healthier life, they do not necessarily guarantee happiness. Why? Because there is a higher health and happiness.

The channels in the human nervous system are the source of your emotional experience. These nerve channels in the yogic system are called *nadi*s, and the highest channel is called the *sukhmanaa* or *sushumnaa*. When the *sushumnaa* fully opens, one achieves perfect health and happiness within one's being. You can be physically fit by doing hours of exercise and even hatha yoga daily, but this nerve channel, the *sushmana*, remains closed or only partially open. When it is not open, your life will still be a mixture of happiness and unhappiness. It depends on your life situation, the thoughts you have arising in your mind, and the feelings you have in your body. Your mind continues to interpret these situations and thoughts according to your conditioning.

What is the way out? The yogis talk about this higher nerve as the happiness nerve, called the *sushumnaa* or *sukhmanaa*. This nerve or *nadi* can be strengthened and purified through breathing techniques and meditation by a qualified teacher. The normal waking state of a human being (as I described before) wakes up from sleep, and the dynamic life energy goes immediately into the mind and emotions. Yet, you can learn how to bring this dynamic life energy upward toward the true Self or Pure Being that is forever shining.

We must take care of the breath. By regulating the breath, we can increase the *praanic* power (life force), which is the essential engine of human beings. You can reach there by practicing the techniques of *praanaayaam* (also called *praan chintan* or *praanic* breathing) and mantra meditation. You realize the Knower or Pure Consciousness of Self that is free from the confusing mixtures in the mind, just like you were free from the mind in the deep sleep state.

When you go beyond the words and meanings that you create with your mind, you experience the absolute field of Knower, which is always there behind the thoughts and exists as infinite Space. Then, the *kundalini* (energy lying dormant at the base of the spine) rises, and there is a sense of immortality and bliss, free from the sense of birth and death, suffering and pain.

The maximum human lifespan is, at best, around 100 years. Just imagine how much activity and effort a 100-year-old continuously exerts to fill all those years with wealth, health, and experience. But how much time and energy do we spend on Knowing our very own Being who is forever free from any sense of birth, death, loss, gain, or separate other? All the physical nerves are made to create the three states of consciousness (waking, dream, and deep sleep states), but you can also open the *sushmana*, the highest nerve channel, and produce the highest state or fourth state of consciousness. Then, you will wake up from the waking state and always remain in this highest state: pure, free, and forever.

How to Eliminate Addictive Behavior

Ten Guidelines from the Yoga Sutras of Patanjali

First Two Limbs – The Yams and Niyams

I.   **Yam** - life-supporting style of being

1. *Ahinsaa* – non-violence

When overeating or using substances, you are doing violence to your body and your health. Non-violence means not hurting yourself or others. You may over-eat or eat the wrong foods or use substances because you feel uneasy, emotionally distraught, or unhappy. The solution is to counteract this condition in your system caused by your self-violent actions. Therefore, the practice of non-violence starts with loving yourself. How to love yourself then becomes the primal question. To unfold the answer, we move on to the other limbs for guidance.

2. *Satya* – non-deception, truthfulness

How do you stay truthful to yourself? The addict or dieter's intention is always to be honest about what and how much they use or eat. But the nature of the unfulfilled mind and nervous system is denial and dishonesty about what's good for you to ingest or eat, how much to use or eat, or how much you've already used. To live in truthfulness is to observe your mental conditions honestly and clearly about substances, food, and eating patterns, as well as your reactions to what you take in and how you feel after consuming it. This self-observation gets you directly in touch with the knower or observer of all your thoughts and feelings. As one practices meditation by focusing on the Knower, one remains free from mind, senses, thought patterns, and latent desires.

When living in a free, truthful state of being, you choose what you need to use, not only what you desire to use. Then, you are not dependent on the temporal experience or high for your permanent sense of satisfaction and fulfillment. From the vantage point of the Knower or the free being, you can pause and ask yourself: "What do I need for my long-term health and well-being?" Also: "How will I feel the day after using it? Is that how I want to feel? If I take in something that I know is not good for me but I crave it because it tastes or feels good, are the few moments of sensual pleasure I receive while consuming or after using it worth the inevitable downside of feeling physically terrible and mentally guilty for the rest of the day?" So, this is the next step in loving yourself. You are not violent in your actions to yourself, as now you are truthful.

3. *Astaya* – non-stealing

Are you wasting or stealing from yourself, your own time, energy, longevity, and the good company of your family and friends by using or remaining angry? By practicing *satya*, or truthfulness, your answer is probably yes. To live in a non-stealing state, you must be clear about what you are creating, why, and how. Enjoying and sharing tasty food and good company with family and friends, we use our supremely endowed human senses, which are wonderful gifts that humankind is blessed with. There can be so much enjoyment in it. But it is also important to remember that good food sustains life and health, not destroys it. Food can be a medicine or a poison. Why would you knowingly steal from your most important and valued possession—your priceless treasury of long-term health and well-being when you fully realize you merely gain a few fleeting moments of fast-passing sensual pleasure? Patanjali states that when fully engaged in *astaya*, non-stealing, all the universe's wealth becomes yours. The greatest prosperity and wealth is your health or awareness of the true Self, which is pure, free, and forever.

4. *Brahamacharya* – attention on *Braham*

Human attention is naturally focused on getting the maximum satisfaction from the senses and the mind. Investing all one's time and energy in fulfilling the myriads of human desires will severely limit the human mechanism's potential to attain higher functioning. However, when you use your logical analysis, you can become aware that these human pleasures are transitory and temporary. You must keep repeating them, again and again, never actually reaching an ultimate beatitude, the result of which is permanent and unchanging.

Those who get completely consumed in fulfilling human desires are ultimately bound to overindulge in addictive behavior. Whether it be with drugs, alcohol, food, etc., the human being, thus inclined, seeks satisfaction through actions that, taken to their extreme, result in dissatisfaction, and these actions, unrestrained, are doomed to be repeated again and again. This is not anyone's fault because if you are unhappy and dissatisfied, of course, you will seek satisfaction in any way that you can. And if you are an addict, this behavior may be genetic and not in your control without treatment.

The great Sage Patanjali thus advises the human being, caught in this worldly dilemma, to place the human attention on Braham or God, or the higher state of consciousness that we experience in meditation. Established in this state, one starts to feel fulfilled, peaceful, and needless. When one's attention is on Braham, the source of all beings, including human beings, one is progressively less inclined to overindulge in addictive action to feel fulfilled. Swami-ji would often say that you don't need to change anything; just add meditation. Because then you directly experience a satisfied state that is attainable without resorting to harmful, addictive behaviors.

Brahamacharya is often translated as celibacy, which is not practical or possible for most people. So, we need to redefine this practice so it can become usable by all practicing yogis. Instead of declaring that one must not indulge in sex or sensual pleasures, we can instead direct the attention to balance and temper all human desires. This can then be practiced and benefited by single and married people alike.

When you direct your spiritual energy to engage in life-supporting actions and constantly place your attention on the meditative state of awareness, you are practicing *brahmacharya* in all that you do. Your attention remains with *Braham*, your true Self, so while engaging in the senses, you remain free as you are already satisfied from within. You are already fulfilled and free to enjoy without negative results.

This state of fulfillment unfolds in meditation, as while you are meditating, you feel completely fulfilled. Therefore, you come to know this fulfilled state directly and know you can experience more and more in your life through meditation. Any other way which involves sensual experience or an artificial high will not last. The *samaadhi* state is your true nature, so as much as you know how to unfold this awareness, you can remain united with your own sense of peace, ease, and fulfillment from within. Then, you can remain needless of only external stimulations.

5. *Aparigrah* – non-possession

Living a simple, uncluttered life helps you stay organized and efficient. You have more time for beneficial activities. A simpler lifestyle also means more personal savings, quality time, valuable resources, etc. Focusing on the essential basics keeps your head clear and your heart full, which means less stress and anxiety. This focus includes not overthinking or accumulating destructive thoughts and feelings. Minimizing the negatives creates more self-satisfaction and, subsequently, less overindulgence.

To remain self-satisfied and free from the sense of lack and neediness (the idea that possessing things raises your self-esteem and happiness and not possessing things lowers it), you must begin to meditate and directly experience the Self-realized state, which is already complete. In the Self-realized state, a sense of perfect ease and natural esteem flows constantly from its eternal source. This state of higher awareness requires attending the Knower and remembering to do that; reading and studying will help. So, rather than only reading novels and watching TV and movies, you spend time reading yogic philosophy, meditation, and self-reflection.

II. Niyaam - purification of body and mind

1. *Shauch* – cleanliness

Shauch advises us to maintain a clean-living environment and, even more importantly, a purified inner space. Diet and activities that are not conducive to healthy and aware living are naturally reduced and progressively eliminated when they aren't needed anymore. A healthy body and organized home helps one cultivate a buoyant inner space. You can remain easy and meditate more often. A clean space assists in a clear mind. You can then more easily be still and know the Knower.

2. *Santosh* – contentment

Sometimes, these eight limbs may appear to not be in the correct order since you cannot be truly content unless some form of relaxation, including *praanaayaam* and meditation, is practiced. But, to master these powerful techniques (described later), one must consistently practice a complete *yog sadhaana*, one that continuously focuses one's attention on these injunctions. For they are a package deal and work their magic when practiced together.

The more one practices *yoga sadhaana*, the more *vairaagya* (detachment) is cultivated through Self-inquiry and inner observation. You begin to see clearly through your experience that the acquisition of things and relative association with forms, as well as traveling to different places, does not bring total fulfillment; rather, you observe that they are transitory and impermanent experiences. But when you sit and meditate you can unfold the true state of *santosh*, contentment, knowing that Self is permanent, undivided, and all-encompassing, and it exists as and in all. You now know that you are not separate from your true Self. Since the Self's true nature is pure, free, and forever, you start to experience your own being as pure, free, and forever, and that brings a wonderful feeling of contentment and peace, or *santosh*. First, you need to be established in contentment from the joy of meditation, and then all constructive behaviors are naturally engaged in as you are already content from within.

3. *Tap* – strenuous living

Things have become so convenient in our developed world that one does not have to walk anywhere. You can get into your car and drive to your office, a store, or an appointment. If you have the money, you can hire a cleaning service to do your housework, eat out, or order instead of home cooking. You can also sit on your comfortable couch with a clicker in hand and watch big-screen TV as much as you want.

As described above, modern life gives us more leisure time to waste in frivolous, sedentary inactivity. People drive to the gym, park in the closest spot, and take the elevator only to walk on the treadmill or use the Stairmaster and ride a stationary bike. Going to the gym is worthwhile, yet we can also begin to value every activity in our day-to-day lives as an opportunity for outdoor exercise. I have even heard that too much sitting is the most significant cause of disease.

Even though technology enables convenience, we can consciously choose to live a more strenuous, healthy life: walking whenever possible, taking the stairs, cooking, cleaning, etc. You feel more satisfied, self-reliant, and independently capable when you cultivate *tap,* which only undergoes hardships for liberation. This strenuous living strengthens your practice of *yog sadhaana* with increased physical health, mental strength, stamina, and stability.

4. *Swaadhyaya* – study for the purpose of liberation

You've probably already studied many dietary guides, self-help books, and philosophical teachings. But it's important to know what and how to study. *Swaadhyaya* directs us to study philosophical treatises like *Patanjali Yoga Darshan for liberation.* These writings guide us to awaken the liberated state of being. *Patanjali Yoga Darshan,* for example, is written in Sanskrit (the ancient language of Indian philosophy), with sounds and meanings based on *mantra*s. *Mantra* means 'mind release', so when you correctly pronounce the Sanskrit sounds and remember their meaning, your mind gets freed from its usual waking state thinking patterns, and you experience a higher state of consciousness.

This practice allows you to achieve a fulfilled state where you feel liberated from neediness and desire for sensual satisfaction. *Swaadhyaya* is, in reality, the study and inquiry into the knowledge of the Self. This study naturally develops in meditation as you observe your dynamic nervous system and changing mind and body, and then you begin observing you, the very Knower itself.

Inquiry into the Knower brings the result of knowing your true Self. Studying for liberation inspires you to initiate a fresh action and know the Knower by remembering that you are the unchanging, eternal source you come to know through meditation and Self-reflection.

5. *Ishwar Praanidaan* – devotion or surrender to one's highest ideal

This devotion is integral to most twelve-step recovery programs as they emphasize the importance of surrendering to a higher power. Surrendering becomes problematic when one does not believe in or want to relinquish anything to someone or something higher. *Gyaan yoga*, the yogic path of expanding one's intellectual knowledge to reach the Self, and Advait Vedant, the knowledge of the Self as One without a second (non-dual), are diametrically opposite to the idea of surrender to God. Devotion and surrender to a form or ideal means there is division. God, the one worthy of your devotion, appears separate from you, the devotee. A highly aware, super-intelligent human being may or may not be inclined to this practice when they understand it this way.

Patanjali's yogic system describes *Kaivalya* as the ultimate liberation, and when one attains this realized state of being, one is forever free. From the vantage point of *Kaivalya*, the concept of *Ishwar Praanidaan*, the surrender & devotion to an external ideal, can be confusing, especially if you do not know who is surrendering to whom. If there is no one other than you, the Self, then you surrender your own sense of separation to unite your awareness with the highest aspect of You, which is Self. In this act of ultimate union, you are ultimately released from your individual, dualistic mind and expanded into the liberating knowledge of the Whole. So, you are not surrendering but, in effect, re-merging with that which you always have been—your very own true Self!

The practice of *Ishwar Praanidaan* empowers people to realize their greatness, wholeness, and completeness while simultaneously acknowledging that the individual mind of a human being is limited and incomplete. Since now you know that You, the Self, are not confined to the human mind, you can, through meditation and its resulting state of *samaadhi* (perfect oneness), purify the human mind and intellect always to remember one's source as Self which is pure, free and forever.

When you have established yourself in this awareness, you know that you are completely fulfilled and free because you are one with God or the higher power. This type of knowledge is what is truly meant by surrender. However, when you have not achieved this awareness in your meditation, seeing the Self outside of your limited small self and surrendering to that higher Self is valid and helpful.

The Vision of Oneness

Peace Alone is Everywhere

As soon as we open our eyes, we become aware of all the separate forms around us. We become aware of our bodies, which appear separate from other bodies. Therefore, the concept that we are all one can confuse the beginning meditator. The system of yogic philosophy called Advaita Vedant, with writings by Shankaracharya, the great yogi Sages, and others, is that all is one reality without any division. One without a second!

If we examine this further, we know that before birth, when we were in the womb, we were one with our mother as we were the same body, but as soon as we are born, our body becomes separate from our mother's body. At that point, we become an individual person. As infants, we did not know ourselves as separate, but we were quickly told: "These are your eyes, these are your ears, this is your mouth, and this is your name." Then, we are told that the body, mind, and personality are who we are and that we have a mind that must develop through studying and learning.

When you go to school, you are told that you have a mind and a brain and that some students are more intelligent than others. You are told that you are a person with a name given to your form, and by this name, you are called every day for attendance. You are advised to listen, study, and do well on the tests to evaluate how studious or intelligent you are. You must work hard to retain and memorize the information that is being presented. At the end of the semester, you get a report card to let you know how you have progressed and alert your parents to your success or failure. If you do well, you are considered successful, and if you get a "D," you are told you failed. From this failure, you may conclude that you are dumb. It soon becomes clear that you, this body with a mind, fail or succeed.

When we study world history, we find that there have been many wars and battles to bring about peace. People are killed in the name of peace. Yet, the world continues with the premise that somebody can find peace by getting others to agree. The belief is that there will be peace only if basic agreements exist about human rights, borders, and property. From this idea, as soon as there is disagreement, there is conflict, and conflict leads to anger, and anger leads to war. Even those who march against the war go home and argue or fight with their family members.

If family members are not at peace, and if each person is not at peace within themselves, how can their family be at peace and not argue or fight? If families are not at peace, how can their neighborhood, community, city, country, and world not have arguments, wars, and battles? From the lack of peace in the world, we can see that a new method of creating peace is needed, as the system that has been prevalent in the world is flawed. We need a process based on inner peace, or Oneness, and not on division. When there is division, an agreement is required for people to get along.

The new system is when you no longer separate your body and mind from the source. That source is the source of all, so agreement is unnecessary, as all diversity comes from one source. For example, all the different aspects of water, such as bubbles, steam, waves, whirlpools, foam, etc., manifest in the same water or H_2O.

When you do not know that the source is the same in all beings, you will harbor jealousy and fear to get all that you need. Meeting your personal needs for peace and happiness may involve cheating or lying to others because the human condition, filled with desire, lust, greed, attachment, and ego, is only concerned with personal needs. When you divide yourself from your source and do not see others coming from that same source, this division continues, and you can never be fully at peace.

To bring about this new method of bringing peacefulness to humanity, we must first understand what the Vision of Oneness is and what Oneness is not. Oneness is not sameness. All things, forms, people, beliefs, and ideas are different manifestations and, therefore, not the same. So, when we say that we are all One, this does not mean that we are all the same.

Many cultures, schools, and institutions have used this idea by declaring that everyone should be as one, so they think that if we dress the same and do not have our freedom, this will make everyone live equally without jealousy and resentment. But true Oneness has nothing to do with sameness. Oneness is not on the level of forms, bodies, or personalities. It is clear that with seven billion people, each one, except maybe in twins, has a different face, different cells, different genetics, and a very different upbringing, so there is no sameness on that level of form or of individual people and personalities.

Then what is the meaning of Oneness? The answer to this question is known when you close your eyes since the human mind cannot know Oneness. When you shut down your physical vision from seeing all the forms and things around you, you will see the space in front of your closed eyes. This space is the space of meditative awareness or a higher state of consciousness. The space seen with closed eyes is the same space that everyone sees. In this space, there is no division. Therefore, in the space of meditation, there is no division. You have divided the space as soon as you use your senses to see or feel your body, mind, personality, or that of others. In the Vision of Oneness, there is only space.

Out of that one Pure Space, or Pure Consciousness, the innumerable forms are all created. A potter makes many pots from the earth or clay, but they are all made from the same substance. A potter can make many pots in all designs, colors, and sizes, but the clay always remains clay. In the same way, the ocean is always ocean water. Even when there are waves, bubbles, and even icebergs, they form out of the same substance. No matter how many forms develop, it always remains water.

Now, how can you apply this to the Vision of Oneness? We must become aware that we are all made of the same space or consciousness, and out of that one space, there arises the five elements: space, air, fire, water, and earth. These elements move together in various formations and become all the planets, stars, mountains, plants, oceans, people, houses, cars, furnishings, etc. But as they are all made of the same substance, they emanate from the same space. Therefore, they are all space. In the same way, all the clay pots are clay, and all the forms of ocean water are water.

Even though we appear to be separate human beings with bodies and minds, in essence, we are all

Pure Space. Science tells us that even though forms seem solid, they are 99.9% space. Therefore, the vision of duality or form consciousness is mostly an illusion of the human senses. Just like if you see a snake and get afraid, only to find out later that it was just a rope. When you know the snake is an illusion, you are not afraid it will bite you. Your body is like your car or instrument of perception. You know your vehicle is not you, so in the same way, you can understand that your body is not the real You. Thinking that your body is the only "you" is an illusion. When you believe yourself to be only the body that was born, then you fear that one day you get hurt or die.

To know the Vision of Oneness rather than the vision of duality or illusory consciousness, you need to turn your attention in meditation into the Pure Space that we all are. The inner vision or inner eye (sometimes called the third eye) sees this pure vision of space as the human or physical eyes cannot see it. This third eye can perceive all the multiplicity of people and things as One, Pure Space.

When we look at another person with our eyes, they appear to be separate, and we can easily see the different physical appearances, cultures, socio-economic backgrounds, upbringings, education, etc. We can listen to their point of view, which may be like ours in some ways and different in many other ways. Therefore, Oneness can never exist on the level of two. If you only see someone else as another or as a form and personality, then there can never be a sense of Oneness.

Oneness is the inner vision that sees everyone as Pure Consciousness, Pure Existence, and Pure Beingness. With this vision, you know what is illusory and what is true. You see the rope and are not afraid that it is a snake even though your eyes may see it as a snake. Now you see the Pure Consciousness that we all are at our source, not only the forms. Therefore, you can accept all the differences and not expect anyone to be the same as you.

This knowledge is an excellent help in relationships. When two different people relate to each other, the two minds cannot, and will not, always agree. Each person comes from a different family upbringing, has a different genetic makeup, and has a very different experience, education, and life experiences so that each one will have inherent differences.

The conflict in a relationship is all based on wanting someone else to think and behave the way you do or the way that you think they should behave so that you can feel easy, happy, or relaxed. This desire to have that type of sameness is impossible, so many relationships fail. When each partner expects the other person to make them feel secure and happy, this becomes impossible, as somebody cannot achieve security and happiness outside of the Vision of Oneness. The permanent or unchanging inner sense of security and happiness only comes from the Vision of Oneness.

The Vision of Oneness, the direct awakening, only comes when you do not divide the space into two: one as space and two as its manifestation or forms. From this division, you begin to see the two as separate. Through meditation, you start to see everyone and everything as one reality. Rather than seeing the physiological differences, you tune into the space or Pure Consciousness, which is unchanging and is forever one. The physical eyes have no choice but to see different colors, shapes, sizes, nationalities, etc., but the higher vision sees only the space from where it all arose. Space alone is everywhere. When you start to see with this higher vision, you remain at peace within yourself, and only then can this inner peacefulness spread to your family, community, country, world, and all humanity.

When you meditate and see with your expanded vision, the Vision of Oneness, you see One Being. You do not see yourself as separate from anyone or anything. Therefore, this is not even *advait*, or non-duality, because that is still opposite to *advait*, or duality. There is no duality to start with, as there is only Oneness.

When you now see a rope, you never again say it was a snake. You always see it as a rope, so you are not fearful. You don't have to first see a snake and then say it is not a snake; it is a rope. You no longer say that it was two or divided, and now I see Oneness. You see it as it is and as it will always be. Illusion means it was never there.

In the Vision of Oneness, you maintain your human experience of what to do that is best for you and your loved ones and the discriminative faculty of knowing who to talk to, who to spend time with, what is best for you to eat, and what you need to accomplish in your life. You do not lose your sense of the duality inherent in the waking state, as that is its nature. You know who you love, who your family members are, who you give care to, and who needs to be put in jail so they can no longer harm others. These relative truths are not the problem; with the Vision of Oneness, you do not forget them since they are necessary to interact with the world.

They have already been cemented in your awareness because of your human existence.

You do not lose anything; instead, you gain everything! Now, you are empowered with a higher vision that includes everything. If you become a millionaire, you don't have to forget where your first dollar came from. This direct awakening comes when you know what the physical eyes see is a dream and what the higher vision knows is reality.

In yogic thought, we say *Om Shaanti*. It means that the *Om*, or universal space of all that there, is *shaant*, peaceful. When all is still, like when the air or ocean water is still, it is all peaceful. So, it is the movement of water that creates the waves and the movement of air that makes the gale force wind, and it is the same water and air that remains in all its movements or manifestations. In the same way, all the thoughts, beliefs, and desires of the mind are made of the same consciousness that you are.

When you are still or unmoved, such as in meditation, you know the peace that always remains with you, as this peace is at the source of your mind. When the mind returns to its source in meditation, or when your attention goes to what exists behind the mind's thoughts, then there is peace. Likewise, you are always at peace in a deep sleep, as your mind does not waver in a deep sleep.

Peace while awake is a state of consciousness called the fourth, or meditative state. This fourth state permeates all the other states, so when you live in your fourth state of consciousness, you always live in peace, which is Oneness. When everything is absorbed back into the Pure Space of meditation, Pure Peace remains. Peaceful people create a space of peace wherever they go. This space of peace is your direct awakening and is always there. May this peace be with you always! *Om Shaanti, Om* Peace.

The Waking State is but a Dream
All is One Self–Pure Being

In the dream, we see others, but we are the dreamer, the creator of the dream, and we create all the dream figures. We can even watch, if alert, how the inner eye forms a figure and then dissolves it. We see with the inner eye the same way in the waking state with the physical eyes. Like an artist who creates a painting or a sculpture, we make our own dreams from pure space. Even though we are asleep with our eyes closed, the images get formed, and we see all the scenes (sometimes in full color) and the people of our creation. The Pure Consciousness that we are creates all the dream figures. Because we form them from that same Me, all the figures in the dream are, therefore, the same Me.

When we wake up, we say the dream was our imagination or subconscious. We might even try to get some insight or direction from the dream. As soon as we wake up into the waking state, we cancel the dream and say that it was not the reality. When the waking state appears, and we again see all the scenes and people, we say, "This waking state is the reality. I am a separate person, with my life, qualifications, problems, fears, worries, doubts, and some joys and accomplishments. I am living in a world of many other people." Yet for six to eight hours during the night, these thoughts were not there, and during the dream state, we thought that another imaginary reality was the reality.

In the waking state, you like and enjoy some people but do not enjoy or like others. Sometimes you say you love someone, but when that loved one does not do what you like or what your mind tells you that they should act or express, then you say that you do not love that person anymore. You can even begin to hate that person. How can someone love another so much that they marry them and then, when they're divorced, say they now hate that person? Was there ever love to begin with?

This changing love, which the yogic system calls *raag and dwesh,* or attachment and aversion, is not real love. They are said to be two sides of the same coin. Because when you have an attachment to someone or something that doesn't make you feel secure any longer, then you can have an aversion to the person or things. This type of love is invalid, as it is temporary and changing.

When you close your eyes, what you see and call the world disappears. When you open your eyes, the forms and figures reappear, and the world reappears for you. When you are in a deep sleep, the mind does not function the same way as it did in the waking state. You have no problems, pains, joys, successes, or failures in deep sleep. Yet, you are not dead. If someone calls your name or when flies buzz around your head, you will wake up and tend to it. So, you, the Pure Awareness, are always there, and that Pure Awareness puts you to sleep and wakes you up in the morning. Without your conscious mind deciding to do it, your heart beats, blood flows, and food digests. So, who is that you that is doing it all? You, the Pure Awareness or Pure Consciousness, are in deep sleep.

You are there in the dream and the waking state. You alone are forever present as the Pure Awareness that you are. That You, or Me, is who we indeed are and not just the mind and personality that forms only in the waking state and begins to say that I am doing it all.

I remember when my father was in bed at Hospice during his final days. His ego mechanism, which was so strong throughout his life, could no longer keep itself active. He now just emanated Pure Space alone. At that time, I had the most fantastic connection with the Being he always was. I could be with him, the purity of consciousness, without the traps of the ego-identity that was making itself a separate person. I could drop all my preconceived ideas of who he was, what he did right and wrong, how I was judged or loved, and what I thought I wanted or needed from him. I could let go even of the wish that he should live longer in the physical form. In those moments, we knew the immortality that he is, and I am, the One Being that we indeed are as One space of Pure Love. We were no longer just father and daughter; we were no longer separate; we were One!

From this, the awareness dawned that everyone, including myself, behind the ego and personality–is the same Being–One alone. When you tune into that Being that we all are, you can accept and even enjoy all the diversity of personality. You remain tuned into the Oneness that unites us all in the true space of pure love, which we all are, and that true love is unchanging.

True love is not like the attachment we know in romantic love. When love is only romantic, you need to get your needs met to keep loving. When your wants and needs are unmet, love can turn to hate.

That kind of love is just attachment; its opposite is just around the corner: aversion from the one you said you loved. This aversion can happen for a few minutes, hours, days, or forever. But true love doesn't change. It is your true nature, forever unchanging.

You can only know true love when you do not need something from the person for your fulfillment. Only when you feel truly fulfilled, by Knowing your true Self, can you see your lover as your own Self and love the love you both are. Only with true love can a relationship truly work. When you focus on the love that united you and stop trying to make both minds, that are two minds, agree with each other. Since two minds cannot always agree, it's impossible to have love if a relationship is based only on mental agreement. When you don't see a relationship based on two individuals but instead know the One Being alone, then you experience true love.

I always wondered why people love movies so much and enjoy all the diverse characters, whether good or bad, kind or evil, violent or helpful. People love watching all kinds of movies. In the same way, the show of the divine consciousness manifests all the diversity in the waking state so that we can enjoy our own show.

If everyone was the same, or how your mind thinks that they should be, it would not be a good show, and you would not like it. You would quickly become bored with it. Everyone would be just like you, so you would not be interested. You would change the channel or create some other drama. Therefore, why not enjoy the show's diversity and people playing their roles so well? You can only do this when you know the source of who you are; your true source is already fulfilled, and it is the same in all beings. Then, you do not need anything from anyone, so you can live in freedom without trying to change others so that they can make you happy. You still seek help from others when you need or want it, but you are not dependent on it for all your happiness.

Like the dream state, the waking state is all the creative intelligence's imagination or movie, just like the dream state is the creative intelligence's imagination or dream. All the multitudes of apparent forms, figures, scenes, and personalities are the creation of the Pure Being. They are all the show, appearing from and sustained by the One Being. When you know that it is all the same Me, you know that Me is alone everywhere. It is all the creation of the Self, and all is perfect when you do not divide the consciousness and say that the forms are separate and real. Instead, you accept people as they are, enjoy the diversity in action, and remain tuned into the unchanging source.

You can play the waking state's drama as a good actor, or actress would play their role and enjoy it all. You can now create a movie of joy, love, harmony, and goodwill. You cannot mentally grasp this state of higher awareness or figure it out with your mind and thoughts, which are forever changing. But when you close your eyes in meditation, you have the direct experience of your true, unchanging Self, the fourth state of consciousness, or the meditative awareness called–*turiya awastaa*–in Sanskrit. In meditation, the world and forms all dissolve, and you become aware that all is the show of consciousness, and You forever remain as the vastness of that Pure Space. You alone are everyone, everything, everywhere, the Knower that knows the Pure Knower,

which is Pure Knowingness. All is One Self–Pure Being.

The Fulfilled State
Freedom from Cravings and Desires

When the waking state of consciousness arises in the morning, and you become an individual limited to the body, mind, emotions, and experiences of the senses, there is no choice but to sometimes experience a sense of lack of fulfillment. You will desire what the senses want and crave because the mind promises you happiness, peacefulness, and fulfillment when your senses are satisfied. Seeking satisfaction through the senses has been taught to you by society and parents and then practiced for many years.

When you desire ice cream, you remember that while eating it in the past, you felt free from all other thoughts and felt a sense of satisfaction or freedom from craving anything else. Then, the next time that you feel hot on a summer's day, you will remember the ice cream and crave it again to fulfill that desire and feel satisfied for some time.

When you were with a lover or friend and experienced the bliss of the Self through uniting with that person, either mentally or physically, you would desire to see that person again to have that experience, which had created a temporary fulfilled state. As the fulfilled state arose in those situations, your mind and memory set it up as if it were the ice cream or the person who brought you that satisfaction.

Then, understandably, you need that thing or person again to feel satisfied. However, what you experience briefly in those moments of fulfillment is your own state of inner peacefulness. If your inner fulfillment was not there and you were not there to experience it, then you would have no peacefulness or fulfilled state. When you are in deep sleep, this is known, as you are not able to experience pleasure, even if someone you love is sleeping right next to you.

The yogic tradition discusses three states of consciousness that all human beings experience: waking, dreaming, and deep sleep. When you are in a deep sleep state, you do not experience anything, so you are not fulfilled or unfulfilled. When you are in the dream state, you experience illusory images, sometimes positive, sometimes negative. However, human beings' life is in the waking state, not the other two states.

The only solution to the fluctuations of the waking state consciousness and the craving for satisfaction through external things and forms is to get free from the waking state. If you are in the waking state, the only option is to seek fulfillment when feeling unfulfilled. Because of your own experiences of fulfilling your cravings through the satisfaction of your external sensory desires, you developed a habit of always looking externally for fulfillment. Nothing is wrong with this, as this is how the human system functions. You are taught to abide by this human functioning.

Even though your true nature is a state of fulfillment and happiness, you will keep seeking fulfillment in the waking state until you are satisfied and again experience your true nature by satisfying your desires. Soon, you may realize through meditation that in the waking state, you will never achieve total fulfillment, as unchanging or complete fulfillment is not the nature of the waking state.

In the waking state, you are sometimes happy, un-happy, fulfilled, and unfulfilled. In the waking state, you have no choice but to enjoy things when they go your way and then suffer when they do not. You enjoy yourself when you fulfill your desires and aspirations and suffer when you are in pain, mental or physical. This up-and-down state occurs in the waking state, as this is the nature of the waking state of consciousness. So, just like you cannot expect that your arms will see, or your eyes will physically touch someone, in the same way, you cannot expect that in the waking state of consciousness, you will have total peace, joy, love, and a fulfilled state. Total fulfillment does not exist in the waking state.

When you begin to meditate, you become aware of a fourth state of consciousness. This fourth state of consciousness, also called the *turiya* state, is the state of meditative awareness. In this state of consciousness, you experience the bliss of your own Being. When this state of blissfulness is known, there is a sense of total fulfillment.

Those who do not practice meditation only live in the other three states of consciousness: waking, dreaming, and deep sleep. When you are in the fourth state of consciousness, you are alert and aware, but your mind absorbs into the pure space behind your thoughts. For example, when a bubble merges with the ocean, there is no more bubble; it is only the ocean. In the same way, when your thoughts merge into pure space or Pure Consciousness, which is behind every thought and perception, you are in the fourth state of consciousness. Therefore, you must elicit that fourth state, free from all questions, doubts, fears, or a sense of lack. Until you reach this fourth state of awareness, human emotions and the lack of total fulfillment will trouble you.

When you meditate on the Knower, free from waking state consciousness, you begin to see with an inner eye. With the physical eyes, you see forms in front of you. The inner eye sees one Being, one space, one love, one unchanging state of peace. Unless you are in the fourth state, you will continue to only see with your physical eyes. Then, you will live in a changing emotional and physical state with happiness, un- happiness, success, and failure. When you are in the fourth state, you remain fulfilled and free re- gardless of what is happening in your life. By prac- ticing meditation and eliciting the fourth state of consciousness, you can remain peaceful and free.

When you find yourself in the waking state, the only solution is to elicit the fourth state and bring about the freedom and joy that is always waiting for you behind all the waking state thoughts and emotions. Meditate on the Knower and observe the free state that remains when all the thoughts and feelings dis- solve into the ocean of Pure Consciousness. That free state is Pure Awareness, and you are pure, free, and forever!

Why is it so Hard to be Happy and Enjoy Life

Two Steps to Unending Happiness

Everyone wants to feel loved, supported, easy, and happy with life. However, very few people consistently have these feelings in their lives. Many means and activities have been developed and practiced in an attempt to live life happily. Most people believe that having good relationships, earning enough money, and acquiring all the comforts that money can buy will allow them to succeed in having a good life. Many people struggle unsuccessfully their whole lives to secure these things. Others attain these things yet still suffer as they are afraid they might lose them or encounter other problems with managing their money and material possessions.

To begin with, we need to be aware that the Western prescription for happiness, as stated above, has failed. People who subscribe to those ways will have moments of joy and periods of unhappiness, struggle, and suffering. When the futility of this Western prescription for happiness is acknowledged, then there is a chance to understand its failings and to look for the prescription that will work. Here are two steps to unending happiness according to the yogic system.

1. Be aware that when you are in deep sleep, none of your problems exist.

The awareness of knowing your true Self is the key to unlocking the knot of suffering that binds you.

When you are asleep, you do not suffer or feel any pain; this makes it clear that the suffering is caused by the thoughts in your mind when you are awake. These thoughts in the waking state create feelings in the body such as fear, worry, anxiety, and depression. These painful feelings may then create suffering in the physical body. You may cry or feel tightness, tension, or pain in the body, leading to poor digestion and illness. Therefore, you must work with your mind in the waking state to be free from suffering. You must break the habit you developed throughout your entire life of identifying with your thoughts as your only truth and open to an enlightened vision or awareness. With this enlightened awareness, you will come to know your true Self.

2. Remain in the deep sleep of your mind's disturbing thoughts while awake.

Meditation is similar to a deep sleep of the mind, but you remain super conscious of yourself without believing in your mind's thoughts as your only truth. You view your thoughts as waves of perception that come and go but remain at the source of your thinking. You are at that source, where all the thoughts arise and dissolve. That Pure You is not a victim of your mind's thoughts because that Pure You is forever blissful, just like you always are in deep sleep. With this knowledge, you can use your mind as an instrument to perceive the world, but now, you have become the master, so the mind does not bind you. With this mastery, you are guided and directed by the mind's source, the higher Self.

The key to this practice is meditation, which allows you to know yourself as the knower of the thoughts, not the thoughts. Thoughts are changing, and You, the Knower, never change. Daily meditation and Self-inquiry into the Knower will allow you to be, as if, asleep while awake. You are not physically asleep like in the deep sleep state, as you are awake and active and have much more energy. You are asleep to identifying with the negative thoughts and emotions, such as self-doubt, fear, anger, and sadness, which drain your energy.

These thoughts will still come and go, so it is not that you must ignore them. Instead, you see them as they are, just waves of perception. When you de-identify with your mind and thoughts, you become the free Master. Only when you begin to identify with your limited body, mind, and thoughts and think that is all you are do you forget the vast and free Being you genuinely are. It is because of this identification with your mind and body that you suffer. To end your suffering and remain happy all the time, know your true Self, who is already forever delighted. Knowing the Self is the secret to true happiness, an enlightening journey of Self-discovery.

The knowledge of your true Self becomes your direct experience through your continued meditation and yogic practices. These practices include discrimination between what the mind is and what your true nature is and the renouncing of all ignorance of the Self.

This awareness unfolds when you place your attention on the Knower. You will support and develop this practice by reading books or articles like this and listening to talks on the highest knowledge. Spending time wisely by engaging your mind in the highest knowledge will allow you to know the solution state of consciousness. By dwelling on the problems in your mind, you will find only limited solutions, as your mind is limited and constantly changing.

The Self that you are is forever unchanging, pure, free, and blissful. When you practice this, you become it. Just as you practiced and acquired the skills of walking, talking, writing, and reading as a child, you can now develop the ability to know your true Self through meditation.

You, your true Self, is not bound by the limitation of your mind and thoughts. Through meditation on the Knower, your thinking becomes purified, and you no longer generate many depressive, destructive thoughts like you did before. Your clarity of understanding and knowledge shines, and you begin to shine. You look younger and more attractive because you have more vitality and energy.

It is difficult to remain happy and enjoy your life when you are a victim of your mind and thoughts, which are forever changing. When you identify with a disturbing thought, you will suffer. You have practiced this identification all your life, so you have become this limited human being with the potential for suffering and happiness.

This lower level of awareness is not your fault as it is what society prescribed, and you followed it. Practicing meditation allows you to de-identify with your changing thoughts and to identify with your true Self that is forever free and peaceful. By practicing and mastering this higher awareness, you can live your life happily.

How to Overcome Destructive Thinking

Beginning meditators usually struggle with the idea that they want to meditate but they cannot find the time or energy to do it. Most people are busy in life making money, raising a family, etc. Meditators often think that they are not practicing enough. Similarly, when you are on an exercise or weight loss program, you may think that even though you were good for a week, you slipped from your program after that. Then there can be self-degradation, frustration and even giving-up on the program.

Sage Patanjali makes it clear that the nature of the mind is to generate thoughts. Since the mind keeps generating thoughts, it is up to you which ones you give attention to and believe in and which ones you discard. You cannot stop the mind from thinking, as this is its nature. But, if your thinking is destructive and not helpful, then you have the power to counteract those thoughts. When you think you haven't meditated enough, bring in the thought that even one meditation is of great benefit and should be appreciated positively.

When you overeat or eat unhealthy foods and think badly of yourself, cultivate the thought that, through awareness of your destructive thinking, you develop the power to change it. This awareness of yourself is, in and of itself, a positive achievement. First there's awareness, then you develop the power to change your thought and from that you change your behavioral patterns.

Immediately after the discussion on the *yam*s and *niyam*s, purification techniques, Patanjali brings in a very important and useful idea in Chapter 2, Verses 33 and 34 - *Vitark abaandhanay pratipaksha bhaavanam:* When undesirable thoughts appear to encumber one's *saadhanaa*, or yogic practice, one should cultivate desirable thoughts which will neutralize that negativity. To neutralize disturbing thoughts, one should cultivate *pratipaksha bhaavana*, the sense of reversing the focus of one's thinking or bringing in the opposite thought. Due to lust, greed, and attachment one can develop a mind sense that generates the quality of thinking based on these destructive ideas.

If one has not developed himself in meditation practice, then the purification techniques given in the *yam*s and *niyam* are essential. If the person's mind is not yet purified, or free from lust, greed, and attachment, then he or she will be subject to that realm of thinking, and it will be difficult to practice the purification methods prescribed by Patanjali. Therefore, this verse is inserted right after the description of the injunctions and observances for purification and before the actual description for each individual method, so you can know how to counteract any limiting thoughts in your mind that prevent you from doing your practice.

How can you be aware of your thinking? First, you need to become aware that you are the knower of your thoughts and not the victim of them. You do not have to act on them unless you, the Knower, decides to. When the thoughts are of appreciation, and you make a positive change in your behavior–reward and appreciate your efforts.

This type of supportive encouragement of healthy living will generate more power to continue doing it. Rather than focusing on the times you neglect your meditation, exercise or diet program and feel bad about it, reinforce your positive thoughts and behavior. Reading this article is one of the positive steps in this evolution. Contemplation and practice will take you even further. You'll become aware that your ability to make changes is now unfolding from the infinite power generated in meditation.

It would be an endless process to try and shape your thinking to be positive all the time, so you also need another method to overcome destructive thinking. Negative thoughts, by themselves, are not destructive unless you, the Self, identify with them and believe them to be true. They are a problem only when you give them energy and power. If you see them, instead, as waves of perception, then you, the Knower, has the choice to act on them or just let them dissolve back into their source–the very ocean of Pure Consciousness.

When you follow a thought back to its source you become aware that it came from pure space or consciousness. By remaining aware of yourself as the knower of your thoughts, through the meditation practice, you become aware of yourself as forever pure and not identified with your mind or its thinking. You purify your mind from its tendency to dwell on negative reactions and you gain the ability to master your mind, senses and life. Now your habit patterns begin to change effortlessly and easily.

Through meditation on the Knower, you have the direct experience of the Being, who is forever pure and free. Mastery of the mind is the result. These meditation techniques keep you focused on the Self, and you become aware that the Self, forever free, is who you are.

You are not caught in your limited thinking, beliefs, or behaviors. You are the master free. Then, naturally, you do only those things that allow you to live your freedom and bliss. Your appetite for overeating and eating wrong foods changes. Your desire to not exercise and not take care of your health changes. And your ability to sit in meditation becomes easier. Now you only enjoy those things that support your body and mind in living comfortably and healthfully, so you can meditate and know the bliss that is forever residing inside.

The World is Like a Magic Show

I saw a show that revealed how a magician made an elephant disappear. The audience watched in awe how this enormous creature was on the stage, and then when the magician said puff, it was no longer there. It is impossible, of course, to make anything physical disappear, yet the eyes say now you see it, and then you don't. What happened? The secret was a mirror that reflected the elephant and made it appear authentic. They weren't seeing a real elephant. It was a reflection in the mirror of an elephant that looked like the actual form.

If we examine this metaphor and use it in our meditation practice, we can unfold a vision of the mirror reflection without anything, such as pure reflection or pure space. When we place something in front of it, it will reflect that object, city, river, ocean, lake, flower, animal, person, body, or anything.

In meditation, our focus is on that Pure Space without any reflection. Like the canvas or movie screen before you paint it or the movie is shown. Through this practice, we are free from the changing forms reflected when we open our eyes and watch all the changing reflections. By using this metaphor of the world as a reflection of a magic show, we can make it disappear just by closing our eyes. Then, when we make it appear again, we know it was not there before and will not be there again. This appearance includes yourself not being there, as the form will change and, at some point, disappear.

Being not there does not mean you don't still function and feed the elephant, so to speak, with the best food. You take care of your physical body and individual life as best as possible, enabling you to meditate. Swami-ji would often say that the human incarnation is the highest, and you need to respect all of the laws of nature and see everyone as your own Self. Then, you help and nurture your loved ones as you do for yourself. However, you are not fixed only on believing it to be the only reality, as it disappears.

It is as if forms are there, and they are not there at the same time. When you look out at an audience of people, they are there and not there. You see a form, but they also reflect the One Self, space, that you know in meditation. You see double as your third eye is open when you know this. You see form and no form as one space. Then you know that both are not the total truth as space alone is. That space includes the whole with and without form.

From this study, how is this useful in my daily life? When we analyze the cause of all suffering, we see that it begins with your mind, thinking, and feeling. The very reflection that you call you. The I has no location, but you put your I on the reflection of your mind and body. Then, you must suffer and enjoy, as that is its nature.

To be free from suffering, you can't remain in the questioning mind with thoughts and feelings. Swami-ji would describe this as if you go into the water with your clothes on and think you will not get your clothes wet. In the same way, you can't be in the waking state or engaged in your mind and thinking as the reality and not suffer or enjoy. It is its nature.

What were you before you were born, and then did you take on the fact that you are this form? That you, before the waking state, is the solution. To know you are unborn, meaning not born to just a form reality, reflected by the mirror of your Being. You are instead the very reflective power of the mirror without anything reflecting in it.

Before the magic show of the world unfolds, which makes you believe you are a limited human being. Just like you thought the elephant was there. There is no real elephant in the room. The room has no absolute form; it will not be there one day. It is just Pure Space's reflection of a form. When you know yourself as unborn Space, you are forever free.

As we age, we see those we have loved and known so well pass away; it gives us a new perspective. All the things that seemed important and real to them are now gone. The person we saw, like the elephant, seemed very solid and essential. For them, all their struggles and joys were real.

They worked hard to have a nice life and enough money, but where has it all gone? This awareness gives us the perspective that they were reflections that changed and disappeared. They were never there. We are never really there as forms alone. It is all that reflection from the mirror. And our magic show of life lets us play with the world.

Why wait until your body is burned at the cremation ground or buried six feet under to know that you are not there? Know that you were not born; you are free from all the changing situations in your life. When you meditate on the unborn, you can live to your fullest potential yet remain uninvolved and free from the struggles, even while taking care of everything the best you can. Then you are living in heaven now, as you know you are the formless space some people call heaven.

The Cause of Suffering and How to Remove it

A human being suffers with physical or emotional pain, unhappiness and lack of fulfillment due to unending, unfulfilled desires and aspirations. Even when you become happy there can still be a fear that unhappiness will come. You may fear that disease, pain or death will come one day to you and those you love and are attached to. Meditation practice and Self Realization removes this suffering through knowing the Knower of your mind and unfolding the liberated state of awareness.

Every night when you go to sleep you are in deep sleep for some time. No matter what problems you had before you fell asleep, you are completely free from all problems in this deep sleep state. In deep sleep your conscious mind is not functioning and, yet you remain alive. Your blood is circulating. Your digestion and respiration continue, without any conscious action, and you remain easy and blissful. A similar experience happens in the meditative awareness. You are in a state that is free from all problems and concerns, and you are blissful. However, unlike sleep, you remain alert and aware. You can function perfectly in your daily activities.

Here are the four basic questions that aware seekers on the path to Self Realization ask, followed by their answers:

1. Q: What is the experience that all human beings don't want?

A: Emotional upset, suffering, unhappiness, agitation and pain.

2. Q: What is the cause of this suffering?

A: Identification with the idea that one is limited, bound and ignorant of one's true Self, which is forever, pure, and free.

3.Q: Is there a solution available to overcome this problem of pain and suffering?

A: Yes, liberation from the limited human state of consciousness through realization of one's true Self.

4.Q: What are the means to adopt to attain this liberation?

A: Knowledge of your true Self through meditation, Self-enquiry and de-identification from one's limited thoughts and ideas.

These are the four principles in yogic thought. The first question asks the fundamental query in the aware seeker's mind: *"Why do I suffer"*? The answer is direct and simple. You no longer must suffer and analyze, ad infinitum, as to the cause. When you continually analyze why you are suffering: past trauma, upbringing, fate, something I ate? It is unending and ultimately, fruitless as more questions still arise. So the question is posed: *"What is the essential cause of all suffering, and how can I remove it?"*

These basic causes of suffering are the same for everyone. As soon as you wake up in the morning you are in the waking state of consciousness. The characteristic of the waking state is change! Sometimes you feel happy, even elated. Sometimes you feel peaceful and fulfilled when you realize your desires or achieve something. When your preferences are met your energy is high. Other times you feel worried, agitated, anxious, or even depressed. When situations don't go how you would like them to go then your energy is low.

Suffering occurs when your system is depleted or unbalanced. It can happen from eating wrong food, thinking destructive thoughts, lack of sleep or exercise, or trauma from the past. However, essentially suffering stems from lack of meditative awareness and not tuning to one's source.

When your energy is low or unbalanced your true Self is covered, or in darkness. This forgetfulness of the Self allows the negativity of the mind to affect you with destructive thoughts and overwhelming emotions. When you attune to the light of your true Self—the source of your life—your energy is balanced, and you remain free from suffering.

When there is darkness, you don't have to remove it or push it away—you just turn on the light of Self Awareness and it's dispelled. You don't have to suppress anything as even in disregarding it you are believing it to be real. You just let it be like a cloud covering the sun. The light or sun is always shinning.

This solution state is available to you. It's always there. In the yogic system there is only one cause of all suffering, and that is ignorance of Self. This cause is the ground, or field, from which all the other causes arise. Ignorance or forgetfulness of Self causes ego, attachment, aversion, and the fear of pain and death. It is darkness.

The solution is always to turn on the light of the Self. Removing forgetfulness of the Self or Knower, dissolves the darkness and removes the bondage of your thought processes. You rejoice in the light or bliss of your true Self - pure, free, and forever.

When the Sun Shines
Darkness Cannot Remain

Swami-ji declared:

"It is very simple for you to know that when the sun comes why is the darkness not there? So, when that light comes then darkness of the intellect will not be there. Intellect will turn into light! Intellect is darkness. We are fixed in it."

Here he is making such a profound point by showing us the ease of remembering our True Self. We are aware when it is dark in the house and we turn on the light switch. Then it is light in the house and there is no more darkness. In the same way, when the sun comes in the morning the darkness is gone. If we use this analogy for remembering who we are then we can just turn on the light of the Self and the mind is no longer dominant.

Swami-ji said: "Intellect is so convinced that you are a human being, but I am saying are pure, free, and forever. But you think I am a human being let me see pure, free, and forever!"

We are so conditioned in believing ourselves to be only a human being so even when we meditate and see ourselves as vast and free, we will conclude I am a human being who is vast and free. This conditioned thinking can be changed to I am pure and free and all else is superimposed on me.

"This illusory intellect is a human being. *Maya* (illusion), mind, and ego is a human being!" Here he is his saying that man or women is the same as mind and ego. What makes us a human being is believing ourselves to only being a body with a mind and ego. Here we call is *maya* or illusion as it is superimposed on Me, the true Self.

"Now pure, free, and forever immediately is that awareness that is liberated from this conglomeration." Unless that comes then there is no alternative but to keep doing you s*aadhana,* or practice! It is not that you give up being a human being as that cannot be done. You are a human being but first you are the Self so you need to give up the unconvincing thing that forgets you are Self and only acting as a human form.

When Swami-ji says "God is doing it all" what is meant is that sky or space is doing it. In other words, when you are knowing yourself as the Being then that energy like electricity going through to the lightbulb, lights up the human being. Just like without you doing it your food is digested, and you continue breathing. The human being cannot function without the light of the Self. Therefore, without the Self or space nothing can be done. So, the conclusion then is Self or God is doing everything. This is useful for you to know that you have that power to trust in the Self and be free!

Three Lessons in Highest Awareness to Remain Happy and Peaceful

1. There is no perfect cause and effect.

The world is how it is. What is, is! Often, people try to search for a cause. They may think, "Why does he act like that? Why did she say that? How can he think that way? How can they see or feel that way?" On the level of thoughts and emotions, these combinations are endless regarding understanding another person. Most people can't even understand their minds and emotions, so how on earth can they know someone else's? We learn about karma, which says that every action creates another reaction, and in science, we understand that when you put certain elements together, you will always have the same effects.

When you combine the elements of H^2O, you will always make water. Every effect or reaction seems to come from some action or cause. However, when we reflect on where everything has arisen, we come to a dead end. There is no way to honestly know what the cause of the universe is, what the cause of life is, and, in the same way, what the actual cause of the actions of others is. We can assume or imagine, but that is all based on our past experiences or our past knowledge, learning, and thinking.

When you begin the practice of meditation, you come to know the causeless cause. The background space that you become aware of in meditation has no cause. It is unchanging, so it was always and always will be there. From this inner knowing of this space or Pure Consciousness, you remain free from knowing a cause to everything happening in your life. You are free from the mind's ruminations about how it all happened. Now you are resting in your own Being. That Being is the very love and freedom itself, and it is uninvolved in the dream of the individual life process. The best way to understand this is when you dream and wake up; you know it was only a dream. Whatever happened in your dream was an illusion, a delusion, or a fantasy. It was unreal as you woke up to the waking state, now your reality. So, why do you think the waking state is the only reality now?

In meditation, you are free from your mind and emotions as you are in deep sleep. From this, you can know that the waking state is also like an illusion, a delusion, or a dream because it changes. Yet, human beings believe this deception of the waking state and appear to forget its source, the causeless cause of your existence.

From this awareness, you can change your expectations and bring your focus to that which is unchanging. Then, even though you continue to do your best, you no longer must only try to keep making the world work according to your preferences for you to remain happy. You can accept that sometimes it works and sometimes it doesn't, but you stay the same. You, the Self, are free from all the worldly changes.

The world is how it is. What is, is! Often, people try to search for a cause. They may think, "Why does he act like that? Why did she say that? How can he think that way? How can they see or feel that way?" On the level of thoughts and emotions, these combinations are endless regarding understanding another person.

Most people can't even understand their minds and emotions, so how on earth can they know someone else's? We learn about karma, which says that every action creates another reaction, and in science, we understand that when you put certain elements together, you will always have the same effects. When you combine the elements of H_2O, you will always make water. Every effect or reaction seems to come from some action or cause. However, when we reflect on where everything has arisen, we come to a dead end. There is no way to honestly know what the cause of the universe is, what the cause of life is, and, in the same way, what the actual cause of the actions of others is. We can assume or imagine, but that is all based on our past experiences or our past knowledge, learning, and thinking.

When you begin the practice of meditation, you come to know the causeless cause. The background space that you become aware of in meditation has no cause. It is unchanging, so it was always and always will be there. From this inner knowing of this space or Pure Consciousness, you remain free from knowing a cause to everything happening in your life. You are free from the mind's ruminations about how it all happened. Now you are resting in your own Being. That Being is the very love and freedom itself, and it is uninvolved in the dream of the individual life process.

The best way to understand this is when you dream and then wake up, you know it was only a dream. Whatever happened in your dream was an illusion, a delusion, or a fantasy. It was unreal as you woke up to the waking state, now your reality. So, why do you think the waking state is the only reality now?

In meditation, you are free from your mind and emotions as you are in deep sleep. From this, you can know that the waking state is also like an illusion, a delusion, or a dream because it changes. Yet, human beings believe this deception of the waking state and appear to forget its source, the causeless cause of your existence. From this awareness, you can change your expectations and bring your focus to that which is unchanging. Then, even though you continue to do your best, you no longer must only try to keep making the world work according to your preferences for you to remain happy. You can accept that sometimes it works and sometimes doesn't, but you stay the same. You, the Self, are free from all the worldly changes.

2. The world is not fair.

Everyone wishes for their fair share. There should be justice in the world, your family, work environment, and relationships. However, if we honestly look at life, we can realize that it is not always fair or the same for everyone. Why are some people born mega-rich and others dirt poor? Why don't the mega-rich just give some food and shelter to the poor and then there would be no poverty? It seems only fair! But the truth is there is no ultimate fairness in the world. There is no absolute fairness in life and living. There is no total fairness in relationships. No matter how hard people try to make everything fair, it doesn't always play out that way. When you understand that the world and life are not always fair, you can accept what is. What is, is!

Then you don't waste much of your precious time and energy struggling with the thoughts of injustice by thinking that total fairness exists. Yes, you always do your best, but don't always expect others or things to be fair. Even when you first learn that the world is all One and we are all One Being, you may believe we are all the same. Yes, we are all the same on the level of our True Nature, but we are all unique in our human nature. Oneness doesn't mean sameness. You smell the fragrance of the beautiful rose, but you don't put your nose on the thorns. Knowing Oneness, you also know that the thorns will prick you, so you avoid being hurt by them when possible, and you try to remain with that which will come out smelling like a rose.

3. Things often don't make sense.

The mind likes to understand things and make good sense of them. But, if there is no real cause and effect and no ultimate fairness, life can't make total sense. We like to think that things make sense as it allows the mind and emotions to rest for some time, thinking that we have figured it all out. But the mind can and will never figure it all out, as there is no ultimate cause and effect. When you accept the causeless cause, then you accept what is.

Through meditation, you de-identify from the world and its happenings as you know it is just like a show or dream. Being de-identified, you are uninvolved. It doesn't mean you don't play your part to its fullness. You still do everything you can with your body and mind to live the healthiest and happiest you can be and provide the most for your loved ones and friends. However, you no longer believe that you will someday gain the ability to know things, understand everything, and do all the right things, and then you will be perfect.

The only cause of suffering is ignorance of your true Self. Your true Self needs no sense. Your true Self is the only perfection that there is. It is free of sense and no sense, free of the mind, and free of emotions. When I say free it doesn't mean that it excludes anything such as the mind or emotions. Instead, now it uses them with mastery. This is true freedom that is not dependent on figuring things out with the mind or in only understanding things with the mind. I once heard it said that understanding is the booby prize. This means that understanding is not the solution for a happy and peaceful life. In fact, the mind which understands is the very problem of why you are unhappy or peaceless.

It is only in meditation when you transcend the mind and emotions, then you can move with the Pure Space and not only with the mind. Meditation unfolds the development of a higher mind, which leads you towards the truth of your own Self rather than the understanding limited to the lower mind. Through this transcendence and subsequent transformation, you come to know the Knower of the mind and emotions, which is your true Self that is unchanging and doesn't need cause, fairness, or sense to remain free from the changing things, ideas, and happenings. It can now rest and flow with your true nature, which is eternal, pure, and free! Then, decisions in life will unfold from this higher power and not only from a limited, imperfect, or lower mind.

I hope that by knowing these three points—no ultimate cause, no ultimate fairness, and no complete sense—you will start to be free of these limited constructs and deceptions and know the True Being that you forever are. The Knower that you are is forever free, and the true freedom you seek will allow you to remain happy and peaceful.

Twenty-Two Lessons in Highest Awareness

From talks by Swami-ji in The Himalayas, India

I based these lessons on the daily satsang that I attended. I send weekly to my students in the West and have also included them in the book.

Lesson I

Overcoming Anxiety, Terror, and Sadness

This week, a woman who had just arrived said that although she was feeling elated and happy to be here, she was also experiencing some terror and anxiety. She wanted to know how to overcome these painful emotions.

Isn't it interesting how the mind creates these emotions sometimes out of nowhere? There isn't any anxiety attacking us, and there is no real imminent danger, yet human beings experience these emotions. These feelings aren't helpful and create pain. This false perceived danger will likely not arrive, and even if it did, there wasn't much you could do about it anyway. Holding on to these feelings for a long time will certainly not be an effective way of dealing with a future situation. If you can do something, then decide to do it. If not, why not be free of these feelings?

The First Step

You are already well on your way as soon as you become aware of the way the mind functions to bring you pain. You are already in touch with the observer of the mind just by becoming aware or mindful of your emotions. You have begun to find the way out. How? You have separated your Knower from that which is known. You have become aware that you are the observer or knower of your mind, not your thoughts and feelings. Swami-ji says, "The observer is free, yet it is assumed to be a body. It identifies itself as only a form."

Second Step

An important concept from this statement is "identification." When you are asleep, there isn't any terror or anxiety. What is different in deep sleep? You are not identified with your mind as you are asleep to the mind. However, you are still alive, and your breathing and bodily functions are going perfectly.
Now comes the question: what do you want to do as a human being? You want to get rid of the terror. You don't want to die. Then you have to purify your system, which is functioning in this destructive manner and making you suffer.

Third Step

When you bring in the thought *amaram hum madhuram hum*, I am immortal, I am blissful you become de-identified. This highest awareness *(gyaan)* will allow you to de-identify with your mind and thoughts. You become aware that the body you are not, just like you know you are not the table or someone else's body. Then the body can be experiencing emotions, but you, the Pure Being, remain free.

Yes, this is not easy work and is not for everyone, but it is for those with an intense desire to be free from suffering. This awareness is the only way out. You have to meditate on the Knower, who is eternal and forever free. Then, you will unfold *vivayk* and v*airaagya* (perfect discrimination and detachment). *Vivayk* is that I am never born and never die. *Vairaagya* is the knowledge that even though the things and forms and diverse experiences in the world bring about some bliss since everything comes from the source, which is all bliss, unchanging bliss is ever present at the source of all your thoughts and actions.

When you take the time to meditate and participate in satsang or reading knowledge, you bring about this total sense of satisfaction that is not dependent on anything else to provide you with bliss. You now know that the bliss contained in the form is constantly changing, and the inner bliss remains constant and can be experienced directly through your practice.

Another method of getting free from unwanted emotional reactions is remembering the state of direct awakening. So, just like a second handle on a clock that is moving, you can imagine the fear or worry reaction to a situation stopping with the clock handle and immerse yourself in a vision of the time established in the meditative awareness and allow the clock's second hand to move ahead again. This method has been shown in Brain Wave Recursive Therapy (BWRT) to bypass the automatic limbic system, which doesn't give us control of our fears and worries. The limbic reaction to the event is not controllable, but the Knowingness of you, the one who is watching and in the meditative awareness, is.

When you know this, just like your thoughts while meditating, you don't try to control your mind and feelings. You watch them in a way that makes them seem like they are happening to someone else. They are a programmed response in your mind and not your doing. Then you know your freedom just like in deep sleep when no matter what is happening in life, you are not affected by it. In the same way, when you illicit the fourth state in meditation, you remain unaffected, and then you can know your freedom, which is never affected.

Sadness

Another lady asked Swami-ji about what she was experiencing as she was becoming liberated. She said that a certain sadness was coming to her. Knowing that everything she believed to be true and everything she wanted and desired in her life before will not bring about the desired true happiness.

Why is this creating sadness?

A person calls himself a mind, and the mind wants to function in a way that falsely believes that joy comes from outside. When the Self or pure being realizes that the mind is incorrect, the mind feels sad. It is like losing a relationship with someone very dear, your very own mind. Swami-ji said: "When the Self obeys the mind, then the mind feels pleased. When the Self is separated from the mind, then the mind feels sad, and the Self feels liberated." Through the power of listening to the knowledge (Shravan), you come to know your true Self; you have always been liberated. A little sadness of the mind can never touch you. Those who practice *amaram hum madhuram hum* become free.

Swami-ji also answered her by saying, "Then you come to know that your mind is not you, so you do not consider your mind." You can use your body and mind like a machine and take the best care of it, but you do not let it control you, the Self who is always free.

Practices using this lesson

Notice if your mind moves into thoughts that create a sense of anxiety and fear, and remind yourself that you are the knower or observer of those thoughts and feelings. Then, repeat the mantra instead of those thoughts and notice what happens. If the thoughts keep coming back, then repeat the mantra. Note how often this occurs throughout the week and observe how this diminishes with practice.

Observe if sadness comes to you. Any sense of loss may create sadness. Who is sad? It is your mind and not you. Repeat this to yourself anytime the mind feels sad:

1, Who is sad? It is my mind, not me.

References: Patanjali Yog Darshan, Paad I, Sutras 2, 4 & 15 and Paad II, Sutras 26 & 27.

Lesson 2

Changing the Old Method

A lady asked a question by first stating that she knew that her old method of dealing with life didn't work, but now she learned the importance of using a new method. She also said that she is sometimes confused about whether she is still using the old method without realizing it.

Swami-ji gave a detailed talk and an extremely clear explanation of the old method and how all human beings are bound by this system, which includes the functioning of the body, mind, intellect, and ego. For every human being, there are three things.

Desire:

It starts with a desire, any desire. Every human being desires something because the person feels that they are lacking. Then, they make efforts to satisfy their desire. Once you realize the desire, you will say, "This is mine." For example, this is my car, my house, etc. Then, the thought and desire became that it should remain with me. From this attachment, one says, "This should now always stay with me and continue to be mine."

That way is your old method as it is based on feeling lack and needing to satisfy the desire. Once your desire is satisfied, you experience peace and a sense of fulfillment. Now, you are experiencing the bliss when you no longer desire anything. This bliss is your true nature. However, when you have based it only on fulfilling your desires, it will end because a new desire will always come about, and you will feel unfulfilled once again.

Swami-ji expressed: "This is due to the ego ingrained in every human being because we all have a form, a human body."

Now we see why it is so hard to get out of this old method. All beings are functioning in this way. Even a tiny ant desires to find food and shelter. Human beings want to acquire, achieve, and possess all the comforts. They have a sense of lack, so they feel satisfied and at peace only when they get a desire fulfilled.

For one person, this might be getting the right job; for another, a new car or house; for another, a new relationship, tasty food, travel, a new baby, or a pet. They are then convinced that satisfaction will come when they fulfill their desires. As a result of their action, they will feel satisfied because a desire is no longer present in their mind or thoughts. The purity of their own Pure Consciousness remains.

Swami-ji said: "This is based on the continuation of the desire to find happiness because the knowledge has not been given that satisfaction comes when all is removed from the head. The desire is finished, and now one is at peace." However, this freedom from desire is temporary peace because you believe it came through getting something. Then desire comes again, and you are back where you started, feeling unfulfilled and then desiring something else.

The New Method

You will get true satisfaction when the lack is removed. You must know the new way of removing this lack. Everyone strives to remove the lack but doesn't know that "the satisfaction is YOU. "Whenever you are caught in desire, you are unsatisfied. Whenever you are left alone, you are fine. If you have an intense desire to work and earn, you will work hard, get the result, and be free. This whole mechanism is set up to keep you bound. You will only feel a temporary sense of freedom, which is changing.

You, the Pure Being, are unchanging. The new method begins with this. You are already fulfilled. You are already complete. The same space of peace you experienced when you fulfilled your desire, but only temporarily, is always available to you. You can only have this when you know of it. Swami-ji expresses: "Space was you, and then you were born and became bound to the body."

Practices for the Week

The Way Out

1. Unfold the sense, which was in the beginning. Repeat and understand that what I call myself is FREE.

2. Rather than using the old method of getting things to be free, know that you are already free.

3. Know that your liberation is knowing YOU, as you are, the space, which is always Free.

4. You are free when you are asleep. There is no desire at that time, yet everything is working perfectly. Bring this awareness in the waking state.

5. Meditate on Pure Space and identify yourself as that, then you are liberated.

We have all worked on this and know how this faulty system works. It is essential to raise awareness daily and watch how the old method functions. Keep introducing this new method.

I enjoyed this aspect of the knowledge because we can see how caught the human being is just from birth and why it seems so hard to unravel this mechanism to know the truth. Yet, isn't this new method so much easier and more effective?

If you start from wholeness and completeness, everything else is a bonus and a great joy. There is never a sense of loss because you do not need or desire fulfillment, and the mistaken perception no longer fools you into thinking that only attaining your desire will fulfill you.

Revelation on Nishkaam Karm Yog; Act without attachment to the results of your actions.

Those of you studying the highest awareness have come across this statement that one should not be attached to the result of one's actions. That idea was always tricky for me to understand. I noticed that any action I took, whether to earn money or to cook a satisfying meal, contained the desire for fulfillment from the result - to prosper with money or enjoy nutritious, good-tasting food! How, then, could one practice this and not be attached to the result of the action, which appears to be the only purpose for doing it in the first place?

This statement confuses the understanding of this aphorism. The much clearer understanding is to know that although one is attached to the results of one's actions, these results only bring temporary satisfaction. Even while acting, one should be established in the *Yog* state or unity with the pure being or Self. You should know your true purpose: to know the Self as it is. When established in the awareness that the Self is the only source of unchanging joy, you can complete all your actions by being attached to the result or not, but simultaneously knowing that you are the unchanging being, totally satisfied and fulfilled.

The result of your action may be excellent or not, but you remain uninvolved. Yes, you still might be affected by the body or emotions. You cannot stop this from happening as you have this physical instrumentality that functions that way. But you can also know that you are Pure Space, not only this body, and that You as Space is forever free and uninvolved. If you are not there as you are not in deep sleep every night, then who is there to be bothered?

How Not to be Affected by Criticism

There is no way for you as a human being not to be affected. The human body, mind, and emotions are always affected. You, the Pure Being, however, are always unaffected. So, what to do in this situation? Just know you as an ego is not there. You are like the sky. The sky never minds when the birds chirp with screechy voices or even when they poop in the sky. You are that sky and do not have to give any meaning to the chirping voices or react in any way, especially if the criticism isn't warranted. You can learn from it if it is, but why bother remaining affected?

Lesson 3

How Not to be Deceived

As you progress on this path of the highest knowledge and self-realization, you may think you will always be highly aware and capable in every situation. You will have the perfect power of discrimination to know who is honest and who may deceive you. You might also conclude that now, because you are so aware, you will never get into disputes or arguments or create situations where others or you feel uneasy.

This type of thinking may occur because of the observation that you are clearer and more confident with awareness and should be sharp in determining which situations are most beneficial. Yes, these powers do unfold through meditation, but you must understand the basis of how they are unfolded and through what means. Somebody asked Swami-ji a question on this topic:

Q- I should evolve my intelligence so that in every situation, I should know who is honest and who is dishonest. But no matter how hard I try, I still get deceived sometimes. How can I develop the awareness to be more alert?

A- Swami-ji answered this question by highlighting this person's thinking. He immediately became aware that this person has a sense of right and wrong, fair and unfair, good and evil and a definite sense that he should be able to know which is which. Here is where the first mistake begins because fair and unfair are on the level of change. Every human being will always be trying to improve on that which isn't fair.

Swami-ji then gave a brilliant explanation using this analogy. A person is living in the field of the mind. Milk is not perfect and is dishonest because it is also curd. Curd is dishonest and not perfect because it can be turned into butter. Butter is not perfect and untrustworthy because it can become *ghee* (clarified butter). Ghee is not perfect and is dishonest because when it joins the wick in a lamp it becomes light.

Swami-ji said, "You think human beings will be perfect because you are right, and all the figures and forms will never change. That is because you are living in the cow-ego sense. You must change your perspective. You are living in ego and expecting people to be ego-less. If it is all light, there is no such thing as beauty or ugliness, honest or dishonest." Swami-ji was bringing in the point that you cannot expect that which is changing to be perfect.

Only the light of the Self is perfect and has no modification or pairs of opposites. As a human being, you can make many friends, but some may deceive you. Your thoughts and emotions also deceive you, as is all in the field of change. You can't expect that which is changing to be unchanging. Swami-ji said, "You have to know YOU which is unchangeable. Self never deceives you. Self-realization is the only program to emancipate you from all kinds of ignorance." The main point here is that you have to know that on the level of the human system and conditions, there will always be deception, and you, the pure being, are the only perfection. Therefore, stop looking for perfection where it does not exist.

Pleasing People

There was another session this week where a banker asked a question. He said that since he has been meditating, he has the sense that he likes to please people. However, being a banker in charge of people's finances, he finds, that when the market goes down his clients are very displeased. This fluctuation in the market is out of his control. He can't tell them that they are immortal and blissful and shouldn't be caught in loss and gain. They wouldn't understand this as the people in Kullu know this truth. Then what can I do?

Studying Your Own System

You are a human being, and they are human beings with this same type of system. You can't study someone else's system, but you can study your own and understand how this system functions. Every person feels a sense that they are somebody. A sense that you exist and are someone special, not small but vast. Then, you feel a certain lack because you know that you are special, yet you feel very limited as a child with a small body. If you are aware of a sense of lack, then it must be because you sometimes knew your wholeness or perfection. Swami-ji gave us the example that if your toe is cut off, you know you lack something because your body was whole before.

As every human being feels lacking, they will strive to gain the maximum and never lose. This sense of gain and loss is not there when you are asleep, so it only exists in the waking state. All the things are still there when you are asleep, but you do not recognize them. The person in deep sleep has no sense of smallness or greatness, finiteness or infiniteness.

Therefore, the problem only arises when you wake up. What is different at that time? The mind now arises; thus, the study is of the mind. The human being has a mental system.

Swami-ji said, "There are now six billion people on earth, and they all have this same problem, so this is not a small problem." Each person wants to feel easy, yet he becomes uneasy. Swami-ji said, "Without the mind, you are simply a green cabbage, so the human being is a mind." If you know that you are a human being with a mind, then you need to know how it functions to remain easy. You must know that you are more than this mind. You must know your divine nature. Then you have the power not to identify with the mind.

Practices for the Week

1. As soon as you awake in the morning, begin to watch your mind; notice when it comes in. Notice when you start to think and the quality of your thoughts. You will be aware that these thoughts did not affect you when you were asleep. Why are you, the knower of these thoughts, allowing them to affect you now?

2. You can bring the same sense of when you were asleep and unaffected into the waking state. It is the same you that was asleep. What has changed? The mind has begun to function, but you are not that mind. You were alive while sleeping but weren't concerned with your mind. In the same way, you can be aware that the nature of the waking state is to think thoughts, but you do not have to be concerned with the thoughts. You can remain the Knower of the thoughts.

3. How to practice bringing the meditative state into your daily life. First, know that the active state is active and the meditative state is meditative. These two states are not supposed to be the same. Therefore, you should expect that in the waking state, the mind will churn thoughts, the body will feel feelings, and the system will react as it is supposed to. You can simultaneously, however, be aware of who is not acting.

When you meditate, you strengthen this knowledge that there is an unchangeable You. That unchangeable You is the same even when the body, mind, and senses react. Therefore, stay alert to that You that never changes and stop expecting that which is changing, the mind, to stop its changing. Accept that on the level of change it just functions that way. Then why should you suffer?

Lesson 4

The Power of Concentration
(Dhaaranaa Shakti)

As a keen observer of your mind and emotions you may find that sometimes you are more aware of yourself as the Knower. Other times, your thoughts and feelings are active, but the Self is so mixed with the mind that you are unaware of the Knower. Why are you aware sometimes and not aware other times? This awareness, or lack of awareness, refers to the power of concentration that has unfolded through your practice. One who has not meditated may find that the mind is so active with so many thoughts that there isn't any ability to concentrate on anything. Once the meditation practice has started, this mind condition will undergo many changes.

The analogy of the water and waves is a good one to be used to understand this. The ocean can be very turbulent or calm, but the water is just water, H20. The bubbles, waves, foam, and spray are all water. In the same way, the thoughts and emotions are all pure consciousness.

Why do we give so much attention to the waves of our thoughts and so little attention to the source of the thoughts? How you have trained your mind is the answer, retraining is the only solution. Swami-ji said, "When you say *amaram hum madhuram hum,* it comes from the whole universe. You then have the power of *dhaarnaa shakti* that is Me every-where." When the power of the mind comes up, you

132

must train yourself to know that it is all Oneness and that You are.

These thoughts are nothing to You. Only the ego/intellect gives them meaning and then makes you happy or suffer. You, the Knower, cannot suffer or be happy. It is only the mind that suffers or rejoices. "The Knower is not changing or unchanging; it is unchangeable." Therefore, your source is made of bliss only. When you are in *samaadhi*, or the fourth state of consciousness, the thoughts never affect you.

When you meditate, you reverse the flow. In the waking state, thoughts move toward things and form and divide everything. You will say, "This is my house, and that is your house." This functioning is a necessary part of the mind. However, if you identify with that mind as You, you always look to your thoughts, people, and things for your satisfaction.

Therefore, the training must begin to reverse the flow and return to the source. When you say this is my house, this is me, Shree, this is my body, and this is my mind, you also must bring a higher perspective. Who is this me or I that I speak of? It is nothing other than the very Self, the Pure Being, the eternal presence permeating everywhere. Then you know the Oneness, that is perfect *dhaarnaa shakti* (the power of concentration).

Removing the Confusion

What Does Non-Doer Mean?

Swami-ji said, "A human being gets confused in every situation and with everyone he meets. To remove confusion, you must remove the ignorance in your head. The mind is both conscious and unconscious (*jarh* and *chaytan*). Through the mind, you are likely to get confused." When you are asleep, everything functions perfectly. Your heart beats, you breathe oxygen, and your food digests without your help. You are the non-doer. You aren't consciously doing anything, yet everything is working perfectly. When you are in the waking state, this seems to change. You now must get up, get dressed, eat, etc. You must do things for the system to function. So, what does it mean to be a non-doer?

Swami-ji says, "Doing belongs to our tool. Your eyes do, your tongue does, but where is that you that does?" Therefore, you become aware that even though you are taking care of your body and affairs, there is a higher You that is forever present and that You is the source of all your doing. Without You, the very Life, nothing can function. The life you are is doing everything when you are asleep and is the source of your doing in the waking state. Therefore, if your attention is always on God, the source of all life, you remain free from the effects of all doing.

You Know the Truth. Why Can't You Retain it?

The most common and frequent question asked to Swami-ji is, "Why can't I retain this knowledge?" We have all experienced our true Self and felt bliss and a sense of freedom totally independent from any situation. So, then, why do we lose it?

Someone asked the question." Why is it so much better in satsang? When we are with Swami-ji it is so easy to experience the bliss of our own Self and fly in that realized awareness. Then, when not in Satsang, there is a sense that I am missing my true nature." If the Self is everywhere and the Guru is also You, why is it different when you are not in the Guru's physical presence?

Swami-ji replied that as our senses are meant to see the forms, we experience joy when we are together. Why should we expect that in every situation it should be the same? Swami-ji very cutely said, "How would it feel if, after being in satsang or with me, you said that you feel the same when you are alone, so you don't need to be with anyone." We don't enjoy this type of expression or solitary existence.

It should be that when we are together, we experience the joy that comes from our union in the Space. This human mechanism is supposed to function like that. In good company, you will feel fantastic. In a lousy or combative company, you will not. This functioning is necessary for the human system.

The Knower cannot change, and it is not the human mechanism. The system keeps changing. Therefore, we shouldn't expect our system not to change according to the situation. Just like we expect the eyes to see and the ears to hear, the mind, intellect, and ego function the way they are meant to. It is You, the Knower, who is always watching and free.

Therefore, don't expect that you will feel as you would if you are anesthetized, drugged, or numb to the body and mind. For the realized one, the body and mind will continue functioning, and in fact, you will become even more acutely aware, but you, the Pure Being, never change. Therefore, missing will always belong to your human mechanism but not to You. Swami-ji said so beautifully, "The sky does not miss the clouds because the sky knows that the cloud is no other than the sky. There is no duality."

Practices for the Week

1. When you repeat the mantra in meditation, *amaram hum madhuram hum*, you feel that the whole universe is pulsating to this sound, and it is everywhere.

2. Notice that when you are in *samaadhi*, or a deeper meditative state (after a few minutes of meditation), no matter the quality of your thoughts, they do not affect You, the Knower. Whenever they do affect you it is only because You, the Knower, is identifying with the mind and thoughts and becoming mixed. Keep meditating, and this mixture will be released.

3. When asked, what is the best practice for me? Swami-ji said, "You should practice *amaram hum madhuram hum*, which is my reality and Space. This body is my tool, and these reactions belong to my body, but my true nature is *amaram hum madhuram hum*, immortal and blissful, and you do not give it up!"

Lesson 5

The Power that Blocks you from Knowing the Self as Forever Free

The intellect is an opposite power that runs counter to knowing the Self. The sun makes plants grow and create food, but where does it get its power? In the same way, from where does the intellect get its power? A dead person lying in front of you will have no power in his intellect or mind to know anything. This source of the person is invisible and hidden from our view.

When information comes to you, the intellect either supports it or denies it and believes it to be correct or incorrect. Then it is very difficult to change your mind. This power of faulty conclusion impedes the knowledge from getting through. The intellect only borrows its power from the mighty universal power of the Self (*Aatma*) but then denies it to be true.

Swami-ji says: "You have to use whatever power is in the intellect as it has been given to you as a gift. In fact, you should give credit to the intellect because it has the power to delude you". When you study it, you will see where the defect comes from. The moment you get up in the morning, that is your ego-sense. From there, the intellect is active, and the sense of a problem begins. When you are in deep sleep, the intellect does not function. How can you, while you are awake, have your intellect functioning but remain unaffected?

137

Swami-ji said:" You must know that I am that which can't be mixed or bound by anything. You are one bubble, and the waves cannot be separate from you; that is *Amaram Hum Madhuram Hum*". When you know yourself as the infinite, supreme power, the essential nature that makes it all happen, you don't get stuck believing yourself to be a small, separate bubble or intellect. When information comes to you, it is only information, and YOU, the Pure Being, does not have to respond or react in any way.

The Intellect is Affected by Me

One day, Swami-ji revealed to us how his mind functions. You usually understand that you are affected by your mind, and that is how the suffering begins. Swami-ji made such a cute play on words. He said that Me, or the Self, affected the intellect so much that nothing could touch it. He relayed an experience he had turning all 35 channels on the TV, but nothing on the screen could affect his space. For fun, he also started thinking about all the worst memories he could fathom, but again, no effect. Why was this?

He said, "My intellect is affected by Me." This statement means that his intellect was so absorbed in the Pure Being, Me, that nothing other than the purity and bliss of the being could shine on his intellect. Therefore, the words become like passing clouds.

The realized one knows they are just passing *vrittis*, or waves, and the same substance of Pure Consciousness. Therefore, the bliss of the Self remains so free and clear like the sky that nothing can stick to it. He said, "The Knower is forever free and cannot be bound by any form or idea. Ideas, forms, and thoughts appear and disappear, but YOU don't change."

Common Questions

One fellow who was there briefly asked these three questions, and Swami-ji, as you can see, gave amazing answers.

Q - "What can I give you to show my eternal thanks for all the knowledge you have given me?"

A - "You can give me the awareness in yourself that I did not give you anything. It is all God. Without God, no words could ever come. You would not have any love and affection that can be made manifest. Keep God in your heart. God gives to God. God receives from God." Another time this same question was asked, Swami-ji said: "The only thing you can give me is for you always to remain happy."

Q - "How can I maintain the delight forever?"

A - "Remain tuned in to or knowledgeable of who never remains away from your true seat, the delight, *Amaram Hum Madhuram Hum.*"

Q - "How can I create delight for others?"

A - "Keep the sense that God is within every heart. Then, from your side, you will not hate anybody. Then you will make everybody happy."

How to Not Get Fooled by Temporary Happiness

I interacted with Swami-ji that week and asked: "When one is not yet completely established in pure bliss, why would one not be attracted to the temporary sense of happiness that comes from the experiences and sense of gain or achievement?" His answer was so clear and direct. He said that once you have experienced the unchanging bliss of the Self, even if only briefly, you know the Self. You know that all the things, forms, and experiences are helpful, and you use them but do not get attached to them as your only source of happiness.

You now have a program, which is your *saadhana* or practice. That program, including meditation, will keep returning you to the supreme bliss. You will not need to get attached to any temporary sense of happiness that will eventually cause pain when it changes. However, you can enjoy it all.

Practices for the Week

1. Keep holding the awareness and repeating in your meditation: "I am forever free; I am liberated, and I have to maintain it." Notice that when you close your eyes, the space of freedom is already there, waiting for you.

2. Be aware that whenever you are confused, it is due to a lack of knowledge. Whenever you are knowledgeable, you aren't confused

3. Identify that you are space. Just like the sky, everything can pass through it but it remains sky. Remain the Knower, ever free.

Lesson 6

How do you Explain Amaram Hum (I am Immortal)?

As we have observed, these physical forms one day will change. The identity with these forms is so strong, so it is difficult to grasp that we are, in true identity, unchangeable and undying. Someone asked about *amaram* (immortality) regarding his mother-in-law, who has cancer. He said that he could easily explain *madhuram hum* (I am blissful), but he wanted to know how to convey the concept of *amaram* to her. In his brilliance, Swami-ji told him how he could see that he was immortal rather than answering his question directly. If you don't know and believe this, how can you convey it to anybody else?

Swami-ji gave a beautiful talk on this subject, and the following is the essence of his talk. The Being will never leave us. When the body is dead, we don't want to have it around anymore. That's because the body is not the Being. The person who in true identity is the Pure Being or Self, that never dies, and is always one with you. Yes, you may miss the form. That is how your human system functions. You see the form as the reality, so you begin to miss the experiences you had with that form.

That is an important point, as you may conclude that being established in this knowledge, you are somehow anesthetized from human emotions. That is not at all how it works. On the human side, the body, mind, ego, and senses still function as they should. We become aware that the human system will function in whatever way it does, but, at the same time, the divine presence is never missing anything or anyone. It knows that God alone, or Self alone, is everywhere, so how could anyone be separated from You?

Swami-ji went on to say, "There is no death; the present is all there is. If death is in the future, why make it the present? Just know that the Being never dies." Another observation that he points out, I think, is very profound. He says: "Look in Orissa, there was a cyclone, and ten thousand people died, and you are not concerned about them. Then why are you so identified with this one person, and she hasn't even died yet?" It is only because you know that person to be your own Self, and your Own Self can never leave you. Therefore, you must bring in the knowledge that it is only because of love and the sense that she is your Self that you will get affected when she disappears from the body. Who is there to miss if she is already one with you?

Free Will

Swami-ji said that there is no free will other than that of God, as only God, or Self alone, is eternally free. If we have free will, why would we grow old or die? Yet, human beings can make confident choices in life, such as whether to do the work of meditation, etc. That is the human will. We all may be able to make certain choices, but other choices are not in our hands. We can't make the hair grow on a bald head. We can't, with our will, make the body stop aging and not pass when it is time. These things, therefore, are God's will and not human will.

When we recognize that we are always one with God's will and that it is never separate from us, we are united with valid free will because God or Self is always free. Whatever happens in your life is because you are alive. Without the life or consciousness that flows through you, nothing could unfold. Therefore, it is the very life or Pure Consciousness that directs you. It makes the heart pump blood, the eyes see, the ears hear, and the mind function. It is all God's will.

Two Distinct States of Aanand (bliss)

Patanjali in *Paad I, Sootra* 17, discusses the various states of *sampragyaat samaadhi* (absorption in unity, with seed). One of the most sought-after states is that of bliss called *aanand-anugat samaadhi*. It is important not to confuse this with the *aanand,* or bliss, written about in Vedant Philosophy. The term *Sat-Chit-Aanand* in the Vedant system refers to Pure Existence, Pure Consciousness, and Pure Bliss.

This bliss referred to is the unchanging bliss inherent in the Pure Being, or true Self. When referring to *aanand* as a state of *samaadhi,* Sage Patanjali refers to a state of peacefulness that one experiences in meditation. However, at this stage, the ego consciousness is still functioning. Therefore, this *aanand* is a state of the *ahankaar,* or ego. When one feels blissful, there is an experience of "I am blissful"; therefore, the "I" or ego-sense is still intact.

Patanjali recommends that one should not settle for this changing state of bliss, no matter how wonderful it can be, as this state is affected by ego consciousness. Instead, one can bring awareness to the Knower, who is watching the blissfulness. That awareness will allow you to transcend into *asmitaa,* or the sense of am-ness. Eventually, in *samaadhi* the power to discriminate between the unchanging Knower and changing ego or mind becomes so keen that the highest state of *samaadhi* unfolds. The ego and mind become absorbed into the Self. That state is called *asampragyaat samaadhi* or *samaadhi* without seed, as no seed can sprout again into ego consciousness.

Practices for this Week

1. Keep these two points wherever you go: my subject is to know God, and I am, at this time, ego consciousness. Then, you will not condemn anybody's ego, and you desire to be free from it. Swami-ji said: "Never mind if you slip or forget. You are a human being species."

2. Remember that God never wants to make himself miserable. For that, he had made his counterpart, the mind.

3. If you are confused, aren't you sure that you are the one who is confused? That Self, you are, and that never changes.

4. In your meditation, be aware when you are in Aanand-*Anugat Samaadhi* (blissful state) and bring awareness of the Knower. Watch the ego identity begin to dissolve or become absorbed into the pure Being or Self.

Lesson 7

Who is Disturbed?

Before you were born, were you ever disturbed? What causes disturbance? When one becomes a body, one's nature is to get disturbed. This body consciousness is inevitable. Therefore, as soon as you enter the waking state and say, "I am this body," some disturbance will come. This identification is the nature of the human being. You get identified with your body. Therefore, you should practice knowing you are more than a human being and know that the waking state is the cause of your disturbance.

When you initiate any action, you feel disturbed or not disturbed by the result of your action. If the result is favorable, you feel happy; if not, you are unhappy. Everyone thinks if the mind is happy, one will not feel disturbed. All the therapies are based on this premise.

Swami-ji says: "Human beings identified with a mind must be disturbed. Disturbance is no big deal as the body, by nature, is a disturbance. Identification with the body is the cause of all disturbance and all joy." Thus, the very nature of any disturbance lies in ignorance of one's true Self. You will not be free from trouble and disturbance since you have a human intellect, and you believe it to be separate from other forms and phenomena.

Awareness is the means to remove the sense of disturbance. Swami-ji said: "It is for you to switch it on to the other side. As ignorance causes pain and suffering, knowledge removes the sense of disturbance. In deep meditation, do you have any sense of disturbance or attachment? That is *atmaa,* the Self, and *atmaa* is everywhere."

Love at First Sight

Swami-ji said: "Love at first sight is the highest because nobody is there. It is the instant when time and space stop and only you exist." He gave a beautiful description of how, through love, we came to know happiness, and then we can use up all our time and energy searching for that love again through attachment to form and relationship. No time or energy is left for us to have an eternal love of and relationship with God.

When you love a woman or a man, you love a body. That type of love constantly changes. True love is eternal as it is focused on the Being, which is unchangeable. When you see someone for the first time, free from any concept or familiar connection, then you see the Pure Being, with pure, unfiltered sight, and the love you immediately feel is the bliss of the Self, the ever-free Being.

What are Chakras?

Chakras are the wheel of movement in the body. They are the symbol of speed. Swami-ji said that the speed of changing forms and phenomena is slow, but where the mind does not reach is called God Speed or *pragati.* God Speed is the eternal center from which all powers come.

If you put a pebble in front of the wheel, the wheel will not move. When you place a mud ball on the potter's wheel, the mud moves as the axle moves. If the potter lets it spin, without his manipulation, it will not become the shape of a pot. When the potter uses his thumb and the knowledge of *chakra*, or wheel, the form is the result. The potter cannot make a form if he is dead or unconscious. The *chakras* of the potter come from God Speed or *Pragati* Consciousness.

How To Keep Yourself Shining with God's Light

Swami-ji spent much time infusing us with the sense that the human 'I' is a mistaken identity. Real, eternal 'I' is the Whole, the Self. He shows how quickly we can get identified and think that I am this way or that way and can only do this or that. Inherent in our very expression is this sense of an individual 'I,' and that is what binds us.

We know that certain things belong to that "I." Mom is mine, dad is mine, job is mine, house is mine, and wife or husband is mine. So much energy gets spent holding on to all these things and their corresponding thoughts by calling them "mine." Your body gets called mine, even though it is different from the body you called mine when you were a child, and its sense of mine will disappear someday along with all its relations, attachments, and forms. So, if that is not permanently yours, why should you call it 'mine'?

When you know that nobody is mine, including your own body, mind, and intellect, you'll have the sense that anyone's body is never mine. Swami-ji said: "When 'mine' world is finished, whatever remains, You are. Light is mine. God is mine. God is I. Knowledge is mine. Love is I. Then this I and mine will be shifted completely. When this knowledge comes, you will know I am the Self." Then, you will shine with the light of God wherever you go!

Practices for the Week

1. Keep repeating: light is me; God is me, love is me, knowledge is me, Knower of the knowledge is also me.

2. When established in the peaceful, deep *samaadhi* meditation, do you ever feel disturbed or suffer from any sense of gain or loss? That free state of being is *atmaa* of Self. *Atmaa* is everywhere!

3. See the space that you experience with closed eyes. Mortal, it is not. Any image within that space has the qualities of mortality and thus will change, such as a cat, dog, person, or relation. All those will change, but the canvas, the wall, and the screen upon which they appear is the basis; the sky space in which all these are revealed is unchangeable. See how close it is to you!

Lesson 8

Ananya Bhakt: Devotion
to No Other

Swami-ji was asked to define and clarify this term,
Ananya Bhakt, which appears in Chapter 9 of the
Bhagavad Gita (22 & 30).

Krishna, the self-realized, fully aware Being, uses
this term to describe the highest level of devotion
that Arjun, the symbol of deserving human awareness, should cultivate in his practice. Arjun and
Krishna are two manifestations of the same eternal
Being. Arjun represents the person who has forgotten this true nature and keeps remembering his
partially true nature, which is changing, separate,
and, ultimately, false! Krishna represents the eternally lit knowledge of the Self as unchanging, Whole,
and permanently established in the highest awareness.

Ananya literally translates as other than and is interpreted in English as none other, without others,
or no one other than. *Bhakt* means devotion, surrender, and one-pointed focus on that which is worthy of devotion—*Bhagawan*—God!

Swami stated that one day, even when the sky is
covered with clouds, the sky always remains pure
and unchanged. The clouds are changing and covering, so the sky says: "I am the clouds, separate
from the sky." Ever unchanging and pure, the sky
appears as clouds, changing, separate, and

impermanent. In the same way, the human intellect sees the forms of this world and says these forms and this world are separate, changing, and impermanent but remains unaware of the One who knows this, the sky - Self, who is forever pure and unchanged.

Arjun, using his changing, finite human intellect, believes that the expansion and evolution of this human intellect to its maximum capacity will allow him to reach the state of Krishna consciousness, which is the pure, unchanging, absolute nature of the eternal Being. But Krishna points out to Arjun that only Krishna can know Krishna; only the sky can know the sky! As long as Arjun struggles to know Krishna using his limited, finite instrument of intellect, he'll remain stuck in the dual nature of human intelligence and thus remain separate from Krishna. It is impossible for Arjun to fully know the Self if he is only using the human instrument of understanding, the mind.

Arjun will know Self when he surrenders his limited sense of I as separate human intelligence and expands this I sense to know its eternal source as Self, omnipresent in all manifestations. The one who only knows themselves as an ego/intellect comes to know the individual self as the Knower, the source of all knowledge—all-permeating, unchangeable, and absolute. This is *ananya bhakt!*

Ananya bhakt takes place when the human individual consciousness remembers that its essence is all Krishna, is all God consciousness, permeating all, remembering, forgetting, and in every human thought! No thought or action could take place without this Self-existence. Self permeates all with its I sense. The I of ego, the I of intellect, and the I of mind, senses, and worldly happenings are all just the reflection of that pure, infinite I Self-sense. Without pure I existence, no sense of I could exist anywhere in form, phenomena, or time and space. This whole field of human existence is all-permeated, all-sustained, and all-encompassed in the eternal I-sense of Self-Being. Self alone! Self all one! Self *ananya*! One without a second! Eternal Being—omnipresent, omnipotent, and omniscient—everywhere, in every time—in all forms, in all thoughts, in all actions —in all life!

In its most straightforward, direct form of understanding, the practice of *ananya bhakti* is meditation. It's that practice whereby we close our eyes, open our hearts, and still our minds. Using mantra, good vibrations, and a conducive atmosphere, the I of ego/intellect/mind/body gets expanded, absorbed, and, through awareness of Self, established in its knowledge that Self, Knower, God, Pure Being, is always at the back, at the heart, at the core of everything, everywhere, every time! Self alone is *ananya bhakt.*

Self creates forgetfulness. Self creates remembrance. Self creates this. Self creates that. Self creates the desire to know Self. Self-sustaining the I sense that human beings should be able to do all things human. And then Self creates a thought in the human being that it should again know itself as Self, and Self manifests itself as a meditation on Self and inspires the human mind to merge with its source, the infinitely pure field of eternal I!

Krishna boldly promises Arjun at the end of Chapter 9: "Therefore, Arjun, fix your mind on Me, devote yourself to Me, and worship and make obeisance to Me. By uniting yourself with Me and thoroughly knowing Me as your own Self, you will definitely come to Me and attain God Consciousness."

So dearest ones, continue your royal road of *ananya bhakt* and keep reaching that shore of Self, your own True Being—the eternal heritage and your true nature. You are always the sky, no matter what cloud passes through it. You are always Self, no matter what! The very sense of devotion whereby you know this is Self—*ananya bhakti*—the dedication to knowing no one other than the One Being, nothing other than the Self, never other, none other, never another!

Practices for the Week

1. If any situation becomes full of emotion, doubt, horrible dreams, or anything else seems wrong, just switch to the *mantra Amaram Hum Madhuram Hum* and remember your true nature!

2. Before you say right or wrong, notice the pause and practice the pause. In the pause, you are Pure. During the pause, you immediately remember your divinely infinite nature that never becomes more, can never become less, and is permanently established in your sense of eternal freedom, absolute dignity, and highest awareness.

3. When you sit to meditate this week, focus on the One who is sitting to meditate. Practice *ananya bhakt*. Practice remembering that the one who says, knows, and feels the I sense is no one other than I, the Eternal One. The Eternal Knower, the Eternal *ananya bhakt,* Self—forever free, infinitely expansive, is always filled with the sense that I am *ananya*—one without a second! Be!

Lesson 9

Avdhoot Awareness

By Alan Wade (Dattaatray)

Swami-ji gave me the name Dattaatray, the name of a famous Avdhoot who, many years ago, roamed India as a teacher. An Avdhoot is entirely free from any sense of separation or ignorance of one's true nature—Self Eternal!

Recently, I asked Swami-ji why I felt so different from the person who had originally started practicing meditation over 25 years ago. I have this memory of a person who, though a novice, was enthusiastic, naturally curious, and full of dynamic energy to meditate.

To make a living and chase my personal dreams, I entered the fields of work and relative activity, and I'm acutely aware of their effects on me. Therefore, I wondered why this same person now, though much more mature in his practice, seems to have misplaced the sense of wonder and driving inquisitiveness that he had twenty-five years before. Why? And should I be trying to rediscover, rekindle, and realize my previous state of being?

Even though Swami-ji addressed his answer in the form of Dattaatray, his wisdom applies to all human beings and their predicaments. Here is my version of his insightful answer:

He told me to remember where the body was a couple of years before. Though you are the same Being, you remember the past qualities, character,

153

devotion, intensity, and dedication. Those are qualities of the body that existed in the past. You are the Being who is free from qualities, but you take on the quality of the instrument, the role that is being played.

The *aakaash,* the space, the sound, and the voice take on a sense of superimposition. When a guitar is played, the sky says, "I am a guitar." When a drum is being played, the sky says, "I am a drum". When a flute is played, the sky says, "I am a flute". The sky is neither a drum, nor does it speak like a drum nor guitar, nor does it have the quality of the flute. But the sky, you, Self, takes on the activity, quality, manifestation, devotion, love, and affection of the form at that time."

He told me that now, in adulthood, your childhood is gone. Dattatray, as a child, was never aware of doing *sadhanaa.* He was aware of playing guitar, playing here, playing there, whatever sports you played, or wherever you were. So Dattatray, in the form of childhood, was like that. And then you proceeded further, and Dattatray's qualities, or assumption of the qualities and expression of the qualities in the body, were also known to the same Being who is eternal Dattatray, who never changes, but describes himself to be a changing being. Because Dattatray of fourteen years, Dattatray of twenty years, and Dattatray of twenty-five years, with all the atmosphere, qualities, and the climates and situations which affected the body, exhibited all those qualities or no qualities and Dattatray associated and continues to associate with that.

He said, "Now Dattatray has the body, living in the same dwelling and is stationed in Florida in the business world where business is nowhere, yet the busy-ness is everywhere. There is no business. Business is the purpose of a human life. What's your business on Earth? What for you have come? All the bodies get busy, and in association with those busybodies, your body also is busy and is a kind of car racing with the cars. Driver is seated; he's never busy; he is just seated."

He showed me that the atmosphere around my body affects the body's qualities, atmosphere, senses, and mind. Then he said, "You, while associating with it, say that 'I turned out to be this as I was that.' You were never that! Never that old Dattatray. Never that young child. Being in the body, you must describe that 'I'm a small jug, big jug, big instrument. 'I am a big car, business, and house'. 'I am big relations, big everything. However, You are forever the same Shyam Space.

Shyam has never changed. Clouds change. Yesterday, there was sun, and today, there is no sun. Clouds came, but the sky remained the same. Even now, the sky will not be visible because of the clouds. But it does not mean that the sky died just because clouds overshadowed or covered the sky and the sun at the same time.Therefore, your attention should not be on the body, what it does or its qualities, whom it meets, its losses or gains, health or deterioration, fast or slow. You remain forever the same Dattatray."

He showed me that every single experience teaches that You are forever the same Self. You have never become anything because you saw some form, some phenomenon, the world of changing reality. Everything says to you, "Look, we are various forms, and you are one form, but our Knower, Self, as Shyam Space, is ever the same."

He clarified to me that forms change, and when they manifest, we say that Dattaatray is born. When Dattaa grew taller, we noted that Dattaa was of a taller form. People say the same thing about your body and qualities. You also associate with the body and say the same things about the forms and their qualities. Still, you must remain tuned in to your Self, who exists, as in sound sleep, with no sense of relations, no sense of body, no sense of parents, no sense of attachment, and never a relation to the business world. You are forever Free, and nothing changed in You.

Then he told me, "My dear Ones, we are forever the same Self, unchangeable, infinite, eternal, and all-permeating as the Absolute Being." It is enlightening to hear the fresh, unique way that Swami-ji imbues each word with that awareness. We can remember that Self-knowledge again and again!

If you choose, please re-read the above and substitute your name and form for Dattaatray, knowing that it is all One Being with infinite forms and phenomena. We are all Avdhoot Awareness, forever free from any sense of attachment or association with finite form, limited qualities, or changing realities!

Practices for the Week

1. Whenever you start to think that 'I am only a body, mind, or separate human being', remember that you are always Avdhoot Awareness!

2. When you sit to meditate, repeat mantra with the sense that the one who is repeating, doing, and knowing mantra—*Amaram Hum, Madhuram Ham*—is *Avdhoot*. This aware *Avdhoot* is always free. No

matter what happens on the body level, the mind with its senses, the intellect, or the ego, You, *the Avdhoot Awareness*, is always Free!

Lesson 10

Dharanaa Shakti
The Power of Stability

Dharanaa is the fifth limb in the eight steps of the yoga system (*Yam, Niyam, Aasan, Praanayaam, Pratyahaar, Dhaarnaa, Dhyaan, Samaadhi*). Swami Shyam translates *dhaarnaa* as stability of the mind at any point in time and space.

Last week, a person who runs a yoga center in Canada asked Swami to define the term *dhaarnaa shakti,* the power of attention. She understood *dhaarnaa shakti* as the retentive power of the human being to maintain knowledge of the Self in every moment. Swami said it is not like a photographic memory or that type of retention, but rather the ability to remain established in the awareness of the Self as the subtlest space.

When this sense of *samaadhi* or knowledge of one's eternal space nature is not apparent on the level of human intellect, then *dhaarnaa shakti* is initiated to re-establish the awareness of Self as the perfect awareness that the intelligent knower in the form of human intellect is none other than the presence of eternal Being—Self!

Bhakti & Gyaan (Devotion and Knowledge)

If there is devotion without *gyaan or* knowledge, and, conversely, *gyaan* without *bhakti* or devotion, *one will fall short of Self-realization.*

Wherever there is devotion, there should also be the ability to grasp the knowledge and vice versa. *Bhakti's* devotion to the divinity in one's moment-to-moment existence is a definite path to knowing God. However, without constantly adding the knowledge that the very ability to know and dedicate oneself to God is due to the omnipresent presence of Pure Being, Self, in one's knower.

Gyaan is permeating *bhakti* eternally. *The knower knows gyaan (knowledge)*, and *bhakti* (devotion) permeates *gyaan* in all our practice! *Bhakti* (devotion) is devoted (*bhakt*) to the one worthy of devotion (*God*). Just as two wings are needed for the bird to fly into the sky space, so also *bhakti* and *gyaan* are both required, working in tandem, for our high-flying bird of spirit to take off, soar, and reach our eternal abode— pure, absolute, divine, infinite, unchangeable Being—Self!

The meditator, the seeker of this highest knowledge and union with the divine, by balancing *bhakti* and *gyaan* in practice, always remains balanced, full of awareness of the sacred as a whole, complete - perfectly united with all beings, everywhere in both devotion and knowledge.

How Does Ego Know?

Q: I can understand how intellect, the deciding mechanism that receives sensory input from one's physical and mental senses, comes to know something based on that information. But how does the ego-identified I sense come to know something without this functionality of intellect?

Note:

Ego is translated as *ahankar* in Sanskrit. Hum is the sense of I as infinite, pure, complete, one without a second. *Ahum* translates as not *hum* and, therefore, is the sense of 'I' separate from others, lacking, needing union and completion. *Karan* means action movement. So, *ahankar* literally means the pure I, the infinite being, incarnating in the vehicles of body, mind, and intellect with the resulting sense of being separate, without union, is needing to act and move to seek and obtain union with others.

A: Intellectual knowledge is based on input from the human senses. The sensory information received from both the physical and mental senses is constantly changing, so it is temporal and impermanent. Human intellect is incapable and not meant to grasp knowledge that is based on the eternal, unchangeable Knower, Self, Pure Being.

On the other hand, the ego is much closer to, and is essentially, the I sense that knows I as Knower exist as something. Something that exists with the sense of I emanates from the Pure I sense. Ego I gets its light of knowledge from the eternal I, infinite, unchangeable I, all-permeating I Being. Without this unchanging, all-permeating existence, I, the limited ego, could not exist! It could not receive the very spark of life by which life continuously emanates as form, phenomena, and their infinite interactions! The ego is like a lightbulb that cannot light up the room without its source of electric current.

So, the human ego is the presence of Pure I–the unchanging Being–taking the position that I am I, the Pure One. But for my own *Leela,* sport, and play, I, as Pure Being, choose to imagine myself as a limited form and finite parameter of existence. This newly manifested baby ego starts to walk, talk, and create a whole sense of the world and my relationship with it!

Planning for Enlightenment

This week, I asked Swami-ji how he makes plans and how his mind works to make things happen the way he wants them to. He spoke of non-doership, that he, body/mind/intellect/ego, was not the Pure Being, his true nature. The Pure Being, the absolute entity permeating all beings, is at the back of every happening, plan, idea, and happening!

Swami-ji spoke at great length about this understanding. But below is the story of direct teaching on this subject of non-doership.

Alan (Dattaatray), my husband, had said this to Swami-ji and the satsang group, "As some of you may know, Shree is in Florida now caring for her ailing father. I planned to join her, but not until the end of January.

So, my mind/ego/intellect had decided that I would leave India on a certain date, at a certain time, with a confirmed reservation on a certain airline. I had planned all this, decided all this, and assumed that this would be my reality."

Swami-ji had attended a birthday ceremony this morning. He decided to have the celebrants set up their fire ceremony on our Center's roof-top stage area. It all just happened that way. He commented that I could see how the whole ceremony just evolved and changed and grew and developed, with no conscious control or strenuous efforts.

Dattaatray said to Swami-ji and the satsang group, "This morning, I received an email from Shree's family insisting that I come now instead of later. The purity and directness of the emails affected me in such a direct and obvious way that, suddenly, the thought just appeared in my head, on its own, that 'I should go now, as soon as possible!' It just all fell instantly into place and, without any sense of doership, ownership, struggle, planning, or mind, I knew I was going!

When space moves, the body/mind/intellect/ego must follow! Today has been a constant flow as my flights and hotel were rebooked, all my visa papers were miraculously filed so I could leave the country, and everything just fell into place for me to go."

Then Dattaa said why this was a valuable lesson for him. He said, "I didn't need to control and plan perfectly without being able to change things, as then there would be no life or freedom left in the moment-to-moment living of life! When I accepted the perfect flow of Self's manifestation, it all just happened in a perfectly executed manner without me having to struggle to do it! Then, it turned out that I also received a letter that I needed to be in the US for my citizenship at that same time. This was another confirmation that it was right to go with the flow of life."

Practices for the Week

1. When you sit to meditate this week, hold the idea in your meditation that we are all sitting together in a warm and resplendent room, and we are filled with a wonderful sense that we are all infinite, limitless,

162

and full of enthusiasm for the miracle of each moment in our life.

2. Repeat the *mantra* using the following technique: Gently repeat mantra *amaram hum, madhuram hum*—on each repetition, count the mantra: *amaram hum, madhuram hum*, one, two, *amaram hum, madhuram hum* three, and so on up to one hundred.

Keep counting the mantra from one to a hundred. Stay alert to the mantra's flow and progression of numbers and observe the effect of this practice on your meditation experience.

Lesson 11

Maintaining the Space with All Types of People

A few days before I left Kullu that December, I asked Swami-ji how I could hold the knowledge of *amaram hum madhuram hum*, immortality, and bliss when interacting with many family members who believe the opposite? He said, "Everyone would like always to remain the same when feeling good. You, therefore, must know that which is forever the same." He immediately brought the attention to the Pure Being, which is forever the same. We shouldn't expect that we will always be the same on the level of the personality, mind, and senses.

When we are with people who are negative, uneasy, or emotionally disturbed, we will notice specific physiological changes in our system. That is fine; we know that the system works like that. We can simultaneously remain established in our true nature which is unchanging and always blissful.

Swami-ji also advised me not to see anyone as "other" but rather as my very own Self. Knowing that their ideas, ways, and expressions are always perfect as they are. It is the very nature of the mind and emotions to function in that manner. You can be aware that they are not only their physical mechanism acting, expressing, and reacting that way. They are that very God being mixed or trapped in the mind. They mistakenly think of the Self as an ego, and therefore, they suffer. When you know this,

164

you have tremendous compassion for all of humanity. You never think they need to change for you to feel easy.

This message was freeing to me. Knowing that the work is to remain forever established in the truth, *amaram hum madhuram hum,* I am immortal, I am blissful, is a revelation. In meditation, there is no other, as there is space alone everywhere. Then, from that direct experience, you know what actions need to be taken. As the *Bhagavad Gita* says, you act according to the circumstances. You are never afraid to initiate action.

Now, this might be a difficult concept to grasp. To experience this, just close your eyes. Are you not filled with a vast ocean of blue-black space? That space is you! Everything else is superimposed on it. Therefore, all that changes is not you because it isn't permanent. How can you say that which has disappeared is you when you are still here?

Immortality

What a strange concept! It is apparent to all of us that the bodies of all of our ancestors have perished. In one hundred years, no one you know living now, including yourself, will have the form you see with your eyes. Then how can we say that we are immortal? Swami-ji expressed this so beautifully in the meditation he did for my dad. He said, "This is the end of the body life, which is cherished, loved, fed, and protected, ignoring the knowledge of the Self, which is the basis or source of the manifestation of this life's tree." He immediately brought the attention to the question, who is it that is lost? It is only the physical form.

When all the attention is given to the form and not to the source of the form, then we say that he died because we think he was a form. Swami-ji so beautifully expressed, "You thought you loved the tool. Musicians play their bamboo flute. People praise the flute and not the voice of God, the breath of God, and the genius of God who was playing. If the divinity is shining in the form then the form is useful. When the breath and the Being withdraw, it is no longer useful. And you burn it or bury it away somewhere. Therefore, the God, or the Being, is the one who is loved and cherished." Knowing this, we understand that the Being is immortal and never dies.

Swami-ji said later that day: "Now you can't telephone her dad or write to him, so you say that he doesn't exist. When You call the true being this 'I' and do not think it is a body form only, you know that which is now nonexistent never was real. That which always exists, even after the form perishes, is the reality or the true 'I'".

Changing my Conditions

A lady who had been living in Kullu for many years asked Swami-ji for help. She notices how difficult it is for her to change her mental habit patterns. Swami-ji said that it is natural for every person to think in a particular way and then be convinced that their way is correct. Just like we can't change the seasons, winter to spring, spring to summer, etc., we can't change our nature. He said, "It is true that we are nature, but it is also true that we are something more at the very same time that is free from nature and never wants to be bound by nature."

Swami-ji said, "I am trying to get you beyond the pattern of your thinking. I am bringing you a breakthrough. We are free from nature and never want to be bound by nature. Your pattern has no power. Only you have the power." The physical mechanism, as he calls it here, "the machinery," is bound and helpless. If you are the machinery, then you can never be free. He continued, "Look how powerful you are; you are totally different from the mind, senses, thoughts, and body system, which is always bound by nature. You have to know that the real you is free from that machinery. You are not the machine, but you use the machine."

Swami-ji then expressed, "Thoughts such as, nobody cares about me, I don't have anybody, and what will happen to me in the future, can only be changed when you have changed into the type of consciousness which does not bind you to the body. As long as you are still identified with the cesspool of your mind, you must suffer from an identity crisis. However, you have lots of company because the whole of humanity is suffering.

If you want to escape it, know that your true nature is perfect freedom." Here, he was making a critical point. You can't change just by changing your thinking or trying to go against human nature and habit patterns. Instead, you have to unfold a higher state of awareness and know that you are not your thinking, senses, or mental patterns. They are just superimposed on the pure space that you are. You are always free, even when thinking those thoughts.

Practices for the Week

1. Everyone you meet hold the awareness that they are You. Know that whatever they say or do is perfect. You can see them as if with a double vision. One with your two eyes that see a name and form.

The second vision, with the third or inner eye, sees them as Pure Space or Pure Being. The same Being as all.

2. When you repeat *amaram hum madhuram hum* know that you are that pure Being that never dies. All of your relations who have passed are always with you as your own Self.

3. When you have become aware of a thought or belief that you are holding that you do not like or that is causing you pain, be aware that it is the nature of your machinery; it just functions like that. Also, be aware that you are not the machinery and that it has no power over you. Use your power to know the Self, ever free from all thoughts and beliefs.

Lesson 12

What is the difference Between Deep Sleep and Meditation?

In a deep sleep, the intellect gets absorbed in the space and does not function. Therefore, when you are in deep sleep, there are no problems. There is no pain, no joy, and no experience. You are in total ease and peace. If it is possible to be alive yet totally easy and peaceful, how can one bring this into the waking state? Swami-ji said, "If you can maintain that same deep sleep state but with the intellect awake, then the waking state is gone, and you are in the fourth state. The same Knower that was there in deep sleep is eternal and ever present as the space of your own Self.

The Knower is the very space of Pure Existence that was in both deep sleep and the waking state. That Knower is You. If you can allow the intellect to function but remain absorbed in the Knower or Pure Space, you are in that state of freedom and fulfillment; that is You. A river is continuously flowing. In the same way, the intellect and mind function in a continuous flow of thoughts and impressions. The movement of the river is not a problem unless you say it is my river, or it is getting in my way. The troubles in your mind are not a problem unless you put your my or ego sense on them. You never say that you are your friend's mind. In the same way why say you are your mind? You must develop the *sattwic* (pure light) intellect to know the truth of who you are.

The Problem of the Human Being

Swami-ji had everyone speak and give their answer to what they believe is the problem of a human being. The answers were: ignorance of the Self, identification or *sanyog* (mixture) with the mind; the problem is that he doesn't know what the problem is, overeating, and not seeing Swami-ji enough. After about 70 speakers Swami-ji gave his answer. He said: "The problem of a human being is that he calls himself a doer. The moment that he assumes to be a form in every aspect of his life is the root cause of all other problems that he thinks are enumerable. Doership is the problem.

The solution is non-doership. If he is not the doer, he is not a human being. If you want to save yourself from pain and suffering, then somehow you come have to know that you are not a human being." This topic has been a significant theme this week; you will read about it throughout the lesson. When you rise above your human nature and come to know your divine nature, you know that your body acts and does, but higher awareness guides it all. You are the space, which is the whole, and not the individual doer.

Why Do You Doubt?

When you were in school you learned to spell the word doubt. The teacher told you it was d-o-u-b-t. Although this spelling looked very strange, you had to spell it this way to receive a correct mark on your test. Eventually, you came to trust that this was the correct spelling; you had no doubt. Yet doubt can arise even when your teacher tells you that you are space, immortal, and blissful, even after you have had the direct experience of it in meditation. You are the certain one. Even when you are confused, you can know you are the one who is confused, and you do not doubt that. Therefore, be sure of who you are! Swami-ji said, "Unless you get beyond the human mind you will be doubtful."

Positive and Negative Thinking

A new fellow asked, why can't I stop my mind from thinking negatively? I only want good and positive thoughts, but the negative ones keep coming. How can I change this? Swami-ji answered, "You never think eating should be stopped; why do you think negativity should be stopped? You never think that Dikpal's mind is yours. You think my mind is negative and negativity is bad." He explained this further, saying that when you think you are a mind, you are a human being. A human being always either enjoys or suffers. The answer is to stop trying to promote change on the mind level and remain only human. That will never work. I have observed many people in the new thought community believing they need to change every negative thought or only say and think the best thoughts. This is fine, but it will not free you.

When you are a free being, you can think of any thoughts that will never affect you. Swami-ji said: "You are never a human being. This body is a tool like you have a car. This tool is made to evolve your intelligence with which you will come to know your true nature. Then you are no longer a human being as you are a divine being."

Freedom from the Fruits of Your Actions

This brilliant interpretation of the Bhagavad Gita chapter II verse 47, can free you from so much trouble in trying to follow and practice what the Gita is saying. The nature of a human being is to take action. Why should anyone want to act if he is supposed to be free from the result? We only act because it will bring about a result. I had a problem with this concept in the Bhagavad Gita for many years. I tried so hard to tell myself that I shouldn't be attached to the outcome whenever I desired something. I should practice what Gita was teaching and act for the sake of the action itself, enjoy the process, and not need the result to be a certain way for me to remain happy.

I was never able to accomplish this. When I worked hard, I wanted to earn more money. When I went on vacation, I wanted the weather to be nice on my trip. When I made a dinner for guests, I wanted everyone to enjoy it and compliment my cooking. Therefore, this left me perplexed because even though I kept telling myself, "Don't be attached to the result; just enjoy the process." I still found myself attached.

Swami-ji solved this whole dilemma in thinking. He said that the purpose of a human being was not for action. The purpose of a human being is to remove ignorance and evolve into the highest awareness. Whenever you fulfill a desire, it is just temporary happiness that eventually leads to more unhappiness. Swami-ji said that the human being is filled with *sukh* (happiness) and *dukh* (unhappiness) but really, he is all *dukh* (unhappiness) because even the happiness eventually turns to unhappiness.

Swami-ji defined what Krishna was really saying to Arjun in the Bhagavad Gita. He said, "Arjun, at this time, you are under the sway of ignorance, and it has nothing to do with action. Just like the river flows, the flood's result is never in you." He brought attention to who you truly are. You are not the one who acts, nor are you the one to whom the result belongs. You are the Self, ever free and pure. Not being attached to the fruits of your action means to bring in the knowledge that all action is to remove the ignorance and to know who you are.

Therefore, whatever the result, you remember your true nature and remain free. You may prefer it to unfold in a certain way on the human side. That is fine. You can also have the awareness that no matter how it unfolds, you have always been the unchanging Self. Even while preferring a particular result to your action, you can know who wants it and who the free being is.

Practices for the Week

1. Meditations from Swami-ji

   a. "The perfect state of consciousness says I am not the 'I' of the mind. You are the Pure Knower that is your true nature. You can close your eyes and meditate and know this."

   b. "When you begin to meditate, you are the doer. Do your meditation. You then become the doer doing only for the sake of non-doing or being."

   c. "When you first close your eyes to meditate, you are aware that you are the "I" meditating on space. Then, you can bring in the awareness that you are the space meditating on Pure Space and further realize that you are just a non-doer, a Pure Being."

2. Whenever you act and realize that you are attached to the result of your action or to getting your desire fulfilled, bring in the Knowledge of the Self. Your purpose here is not to get your desires fulfilled. It is to know yourself as Pure and Free. You can only experience this when you close your eyes and know yourself as that space in front of your closed eyes. That space is independent of fulfilling your desire and is always filled with bliss.

Lesson 13

The Fault-Finding Mind

Every person has conditions based on their experiences. If someone is brought up with cows and sheep, a particular smell will be natural to them. So much so that if the animals were no longer there, it would not smell nice. When you are brought up in the country, that is familiar to you. In the city, you will have a different set of conditions. We all know the story of the boy brought up with wolves and how he took on those behavior patterns. In Sanskrit, this conditioning is called their *swabhaav*. If a person sees the sun, a river, and trees, then he will know what these things are. If some of these things are unfamiliar, he might find fault with them. Your upbringing can be the nature of all fault-finding.

When you study your mind and system, you can become aware of how conditioned you are to see things in a certain way and how you can find fault with those that are different. If you begin to understand that everyone has their *swabhaav* or conditions, even if they differ from yours, it is the only way they can see things due to their conditioning. With this perception, you will remain free from finding fault in anyone. Yes, you must decide what company to keep and who to be friends with. You should always find the company of people who love and appreciate you. However, you do not need to find fault with those who are different, even when you choose not to keep their company.

Swami-ji said, "If you find fault just because your habits are different, then you cannot get this

175

knowledge." He pointed out that if you find fault with your teacher, you will not be open to hearing or understanding things differently than your conditioning dictates. You will not be able to receive new knowledge or information. You can receive this knowledge when you remain open to seeing beyond your conditioned mind, which is not based on society's dictates. As people are conditioned that they are a body and mind, unless you can remain open to the possibility that you are space, you will never be able to experience yourself as space.

I Don't Think I Transcend in my Meditation

Someone described her meditation practice to Swami-ji and said that although she feels peaceful, she doesn't always feel like she transcends her mind. Swami-ji said, "You have made a concept that you want to get away from everything that changes that you don't like." He explained how you have the idea that you are your body and mind, so you are suffering with your thoughts. You have become caught in *sanyog,* or mixture, with the body and mind. When you say that you are a body, that is when the problem arises. You have the whole process backward.

You need to come to know the real You before the body. In deep sleep, you never meditate; you are simply a Pure Being. Your body is sitting in meditation, but you say, "I am sitting." You must know who meditates that I is forever in sleep, dream, and waking. Swami-ji said: "The blue-black space is forever. That forever you are." Therefore, in meditation, the idea that you must transcend something is false. You are already the transcended, free, forever, Pure Being. The thoughts are just passing clouds or waves of perception. You can put your attention on the one that knows your mind. That Knower you are, not the body that needs to be transcended.

Burning the Seed of Sanskaar

Swami-ji said. "When you know the Self who is forever free you have burned the seed of your *sanskaar*, or mental impressions." As most of you know, *sanskaars* are those deep impressions that keep you caught in patterns of thinking and behaving that result in suffering or happiness. As long as *sanskaar* is present, you will still be the victim of your thinking. *Sanskaar* will get finished when you remain the non-doer—the one who is the unchanging being. If you believe yourself to be the doer then you will always be subject to the results of your action, whether good or bad.

When you are dreaming, you know that it is all your imagination playing with the many experiences and ideas in the deep recesses of your own mind. In the same way, when you wake up, you are in the waking state, so you are a player in the drama that you call the world. It is all formed by your imagination, or *sankalp*.

If you think or imagine yourself as pretty, you will act like someone pretty. You will play that role if you think or imagine yourself to be small. We all remember the Twilight Zone episode when they showed a woman who was in the hospital bed having plastic surgery. Everyone was saying how ugly she was, and they hoped that this surgery would work to make her beautiful. After they removed the bandages and revealed her face, it was the face of a gorgeous blond woman. The nurses and doctors were horrified and said the surgery had failed. Then, they showed the faces of the doctors and nurses, who all had pig faces. Because of their *swabaav,* standard conditioning, *sankalp,* or imagination, they considered themselves beautiful and what we usually call beautiful to be ugly.

In the same way, the idea that you are an individual doer is your *sankalp.* The truth is you are unchanging space, ever pure and uninvolved with the drama that the mind and body are playing, which you call your life. The awareness that comes with meditation will keep you free, and these false impressions will not remain. Just like the waves are always the same ocean water. We can call them waves, but they are the same ocean. The impressions are the same Pure Consciousness that took on a form. In meditation, they will return to their source, the vast ocean of Pure Consciousness.

I still Feel Like a Human Being Even Though I Know I'm the Self.

Someone expressed that although she knows the truth of who she is, she still feels like a limited and small human being. Why is this? Swami-ji said: "The thinking of all human beings in incorrect. You can correct incorrect thinking by taking your "I" off the body and putting it on the *Aatma* or Self. Placing the I on the Self is correct thinking." Here, Swami-ji expresses how you will continue to think and feel like a human being until you are sure your very "I" is the Self. Knowing that your I is the Self is the only truly valuable type of thinking. As I said in last week's lesson, changing negative thoughts to positive ones is not the way to get free. You need to keep bringing in the highest thought.

Regarding this, someone else asked why, even though he kept saying, "I am the Whole," but this was not always his perception. Swami-ji answered by saying: "As you keep calling yourself a boy and now a man with a name and form and any time someone calls your name, you answer to it, and you believe that is who you are, in the same way, if you keep saying, "I am the Whole" then you will come to know that the Whole or Space is who you are. You will only answer to that name."

How Can I Get Rid of Bad Memories that Are Still Affecting Me?

A lady said that she had a terrible childhood. Her father was verbally and physically abusive. She realized that these memories and past experiences were now affecting her present relationship, and she wanted to know, how to get rid of memories which are causing certain reaction in her life now? Swami-ji so brilliantly took her beyond the apparent problem. He said, "If you have memories, this is good. Why do you think you need to get rid of memories? It is not a matter of getting rid of them but appreciating that they come and go.

You should know that You are the one who remembers and that is a great power" If you try to get rid of memories then you will only remember them more. Therefore, know this is your most excellent power to remember. He said that she should write her autobiography. That way others will read it and she will get rid of them. Mostly he said that the one who remembers can now remember the source, ever free, even during these experiences. Therefore, give credit to yourself for your great power of memory. Swami-ji said: "Memory is a useful tool. When you remember your true nature, that will help you to remove this mind which suffers."

Practices for the Week

1. Whenever you find fault in others, be aware that they are your own Self. Then you will have compassion and understanding rather then finding fault. You can put yourself in their shoes and know from their perspective how they see things. When other people criticize or find fault in your company, please don't do the same thing by now finding fault with them. Initiate other conversations that are free from fault finding.

2. When you sit for meditation, know it is your body sitting and not You. Keep repeating, I am the whole. This repetition will unfold your awareness that the body is sitting, but the Space you are!

Lesson 14

How to be Relieved from Missing

Swami-ji said: "Regarding this affair of missing, I want to relieve you forever." He explained what is missing is very clearly that when you reach the height of Oneness with someone, you remember them, and then you miss them. When you hold the memory of someone in your heart, you are not missing them; you feel good. Even though you are not missing them inside your head, you can begin to miss them outside. You think that you must see them in front of you. You then will not feel good until you see them both inside your head and in front of you. Then you will say that you are not missing them.

When you see a car in your head and want to see it, you buy it. You will start missing the vehicle when it is not in your head. You, therefore, want to create a situation where the forms should remain in your head and in front of you. As long as there are two persons, you will never experience this total union, and missing will always occur. Swami-ji said: "Provided we know that we are the Self, then love is not of the form. Love is an independent reality. Man is only missing the knowledge of the Self."

When you believe it is the person you are missing, you will always suffer because they cannot remain with you permanently. Knowing that we are one being will free you from missing. The missing only begins because sometimes you feel the Oneness with that person or thing. Then, when you thought you lost it, or if it was away from you for some time, you experienced a need for that person to complete your Oneness. Needing someone to know your Oneness is false knowledge. Self is independent of union with the forms. Self is forever one with the whole. Swami-ji said, "If your mind or ego gets dropped in space, then you know Space you are." Then there is no missing as Space is the whole.

Two Fields of Awareness

When we meditate, our bodies remain the same, and we are quiet. The mind settles in another field, which is placid and fulfilled. The mind is no longer in the field of agitation. The mind is like air. When it settles, it is in the field of placidity, and the body also settles. Even when you start talking, you can remain in this placid field.

Swami-ji continued by pointing out that you must know why you have come to this earth. The birds and animals cannot understand this. Everyone says, "I am not enough. I am not fulfilled." This state will make them move to where they will feel fulfilled. Therefore, the purpose of the unfulfilled state is to guide you toward the knowledge that there is a fulfilled state. You will know this only when you focus on why you have come to earth. Swami-ji said: "Who will be fulfilled, the one who hits the target and knows why they have come on earth. It is only to evolve the perfection that they are."

A Very Important Point

Swami-ji said for everyone to write this down because it is a V.I.P. (very important point). He said: "When a human being is asleep, he is not a human being because he has no mind at that time. Only when he wakes up does he become a human being, which means a human mind. Therefore, whether we call him a human being or a human mind, these two words belong to the consciousness with which somebody becomes conscious and calls himself I. At that very moment, this is so true that whatever it will think it will call itself separate from thinking. It will call I or me an independent knower of his thinking, which he will call creation. Thus, on the level of his I, I for a human being is always true or accurate; for him, his thinking will always be his creation. Thus, he will never know that his I is creator and creation, but when he knows the creator, he is separate and creation is separate; therefore, whatever his thinking is belonging to any thought, idea, or meaning, a person will think that is real.

Because his I is real and everyone has the power in their I, any different thought can be created. Thus, each I of a person can generate as many thoughts or sprouts as there can be, and no human being with his I can know what other person's I am thinking, creating, or imagining or why he thinks that his creation of thought of a form of imagination is very actual. He does not know how many millions of thoughts I can create, and he will never know that all his thoughts are nothing but I.

What Guru-ji is saying is a definite principle. Every human being's I is awareness. as well as unawareness. Thus, I has awareness as well as unawareness at that same time. Therefore, no solution or resolution exists for a person with I. "Here, we can see that the very I is the creation of the Self and the creator of the thought. Therefore, it is both the creation and the creator. Swami-ji made this critical and profound point, which was the Satsang's focus that week. All the trouble begins for a human being when he first calls himself I. As soon as the Pure Being awakes in the morning and takes on this, I, a body and mind with thoughts, the forgetfulness sets in, and the trouble begins. He also points out that we must observe our mechanism and how it functions.

As soon as the awareness comes that you are an I, right then, allow your I to return to the source or space. If you created the I, you know you are the creator; you can also enable it to return to the source or space. This practice can be done in meditation, as you watch your thoughts come and you begin to say, "I am thinking," instead become aware that the Knower is watching the Space, and then the I becomes absorbed in that space.

Swami-ji said:" As long as you identify with I, the suffering will continue. When you have more awareness, you will have the strength never to get upset. The only difficulty with a human being is they don't have awareness of the Self. If you know the Self, then no worry of gain or loss."

Someone asked Swami-ji: "What is different for you? You also describe things you see by saying 'I" saw these things. Who is seeing if you are not identified with I?" Swami-ji said: "Just like in a dream, I know neither I am real nor the dream is real. That is Guru. Guru I is not the same I as your I, but he often uses the word I. His person is always aware that I do not exist; only Self exists. The mind will know the Self only when it goes to the Self. All the I's belong to one I, that is Guru I. Those who have come to know are lucky. Those who don't know are also lucky because they want to know."

Practices for the Week

1. Whenever you miss someone, remember that you are already one with them. In Oneness, there aren't two; therefore, who is there to miss?

2. While meditating, notice when the 'I' begins to say, "I am thinking, I am mind." Then, begin to watch the knower watching the space. Notice, where has your I gone?

Lesson 15

Placing the Attention on the Knower

Someone asked, "How can I focus on the Knower when my mind is agitated? Swami-ji explained how placing our attention on our body or a tree is easy, but when we say to put the attention on the Knower, that isn't a form, and it is elusive.

How can you focus on the Knower when you don't know where the Knower is? Swami-ji said, "When you are asking this, the Knower who knows the question spoke to you." Your eyes may not see, or your ears may not hear the Knower. The senses can't see the very Knower who has made you manifest. The Knower is always there, even in deep sleep. When you need to go to the bathroom or get bitten by a bug, the Knower wakes you up; the Knower is everywhere. Swami-ji held his hands up between the air or space and said, "Your eyes will not be able to see the Self." How does the power come to make fire or to digest your food? In the same way, you don't see that power; you can't see the Self or Knower.

Swami-ji said: "Self gives you your breath, and you don't get an electric bill. Your eyes see, and your ears hear, and you don't get a seeing or hearing bill. The Self may not be visible, but it makes the forest alive and the desert dry." This cosmic power is moving everything; the one who knows this is the very Knower.

When you unhook your senses from the things and forms that are changing, you know that which is unchanging, that you are. That which is clinging to all the aspects that are changing can be dropped. The sense that says I am this or I am that is already changing. You will not suffer when you do not get attached. Knower is forever free and unattached. That Knower you already are, so no work is needed; know the unchanging, that is Knower.

The Russians are Coming

Sunday, a group of people from Russia visited the ashram. They were artists who were on a tour of India. They went to see the Roerich Art Gallery near Nagar, a town near the ashram. The director of the gallery (a longtime associate of the ashram and Swami-ji) wanted them to visit. Eight of them attended satsang on Sunday. Swami-ji came out early that day and arranged the furniture with comfortable couches for them to sit on around him. Some didn't speak much English, and one interpreted what Swami-ji said in Russian.

One cute point Swami-ji made was when one of them asked," How can you experience universal love?" Swami-ji replied," Whatever you put your 'my' on you love. When you put your 'my' on your body, you love it. When you put your 'my' on your relations and friends, you love them. Then just put your 'my' on the whole universe, and you will love the entire universe." Then Swami-ji called a group to sing the seven selected verses from the Bhagavad Gita that he had everyone learn in many languages, in Russian. They were all charmed to hear this highest knowledge in their language.

It was amazing to watch the transformation that occurred in these people. When they first arrived, they had skeptical and tense faces. Swami-ji spoke and led a meditation, and he had them express themselves after the meditation. Each spoke from the realized space they were in, sharing how relaxed and free they felt in Swami-ji's presence. He then gave them all a white shawl, took a Polaroid picture with each of them, and gave them a copy. They seemed like the happiest people on earth (smiling from ear to ear); they were now filled with joy.

We have observed this happening in Guru-ji's presence many times. Each time, we are awe-struck as to how this transformation happens in front of our very eyes. One time, after the folks had left, I asked Swami-ji, how is it when people come who seem uptight and very relative that so quickly you transform them into oneness? I asked, "Is this a technique you have, or is it just due to your enlightenment?" He said that to him, there are no others, so when they come, he sees only the Self, and they all become that. Here, we can see the great power of Self-realization as a direct awakening.

Everyone is transformed in Swami-ji's presence due to his establishment in the vision of oneness. Swami-ji said," When you are established in the Self you just play a role in this body. Then you can play the hero and make people happy." From observing this, we can have this direct experience by reading about it and attending to that space, which is forever one Being, Alone. In meditation, watching the space behind all the thoughts and feelings that is always there and always remains as one with all, will bring about this direct experience.

Jonny's Question

A nine-year-old (the son of one of our friends in Canada) who met Swami-ji e-mailed this question to him. He said that he had seen a movie about the world ending and that since then, he has been afraid and can't sleep. He said his mom keeps telling him he is immortal, but he is still fearful. He knows that Swami-ji has helped him before; therefore, he is asking him again for his guidance. Swami-ji so beautifully leads his attention to the truth. He told him that the world will never be annihilated because you are the world, and you are immortal. Movies are meant for your mind to turn into falsity. They are created by the skill of the movie makers to get your interest and to invoke your fear.

Swami-ji continued telling him that you must be wise, and if you can't stay away from such movies, repeat *amaram hum madhuram hum* before bed and when you awake in the morning. You have the techniques and the tools to counteract all this ignorance and remain free. You must use it. As much as all this wrong information went into your head about death and destruction, that is how much the correct information needs to be cemented. Keep repeating and knowing that I am immortal, I am blissful, I was never born, and therefore, I never will die. This will remove the fear created by movies.

Forever Free and Pure

Swami-ji said, "You only must do the work of dissolving the drop in the ocean. Only then will you know you have never been separate and have never been only a human being." He is saying that you are the whole ocean of Pure Consciousness, but you feel you are just a drop, a human being, and

189

separate. You need to allow yourself to dissolve in the whole of space and be free. Dissolving in the space is done in meditation.

Just as Swami-ji was leaving satsang yesterday, he said you only must remember these two words and meditate on them, forever free and pure.

Practices for the Week

1. Whenever you remember, in meditation or daily, ask yourself, "Who knows?" Then, immediately, a shift happens, and you are attending the Knower.

2. Notice that if you place your 'my' on the whole universe, you become that and love it.

3. Meditate on these two words: free and pure. Know that you are fearless and worry less, forever free and pure.

Lesson 16

Worry Makes You Weak, Sadness Inspires You

Someone told Swami-ji that she is sad about getting more wrinkles and worried about not having enough money. She wanted to know how to deal with these feelings. Swami-ji very beautifully described the differences between worry and sadness. He said that worry comes to you because you find fault. You feel sad when you think you should do something you cannot do. This sadness will make you aware and inspire you to do whatever you can to improve.

He said that you should tolerate sadness because it compels you not to be sad. When you are worried, you are in pain and uneasy. This worry comes with your ego sense. The ego-sense is so powerful that you cannot remove the worry. Then, to remove the worry, you get angry, and with anger, you lose your reasoning power.

Worries also make you weak because you lose energy and vitality when angry. Swami-ji went on to say that there are two ways to remove worry. One is to go to sleep, as you do not have worries in a deep sleep. The other is to repeat *amaram hum madhuram hum* with vengeance.

About this topic, Swami-ji also said: "Your worries come without you asking, and they will go without your pushing. I am not worried because I never think I must remove the trouble. I never think that I should make you realized, why? Because I have no ego to think." If you are worried about money, Swami-ji said, " You do not think God is watching over you. Let God be worried about it. Even if you get money you will remain worried. As long as you are alive treat it that you will be taken care of because it is the God taking care of you."

How to Live an Egoless State

When the ego-less state comes, it just comes. You cannot live in an ego-less state with your ego. Whenever you say, "I am this body," say," I am the sky." Swami-ji said," You should practice this. How to practice this is like filling a jug, drop by drop." You must have patience and keep practicing; slowly and slowly, the knowledge replaces the ignorance. Why was the "I am" not there when you were asleep? The "I am" should be transformed into "I am that."

Someone asked Swami-ji, "Is this individual "I" just a bad habit?" He said, "It is not a habit. Your mouth talks, and that is not a habit." That is the way that the human system functions. The Knower enjoys all your talking and hearing. Each human being must pay attention to the Knower. When you have Knower, then you are ego-less. Swami-ji said, "You want to call "I" as Knower. That is the problem."

Someone asked, "How can I be free from ego?" Swami-ji said, "Just know you are already free. All human beings have an ego. Just know that you were never a human being; you are freedom." I have always appreciated how Swami-ji reminds us that our original state is freedom, not ego. Therefore, it is not that we must remove or not have an ego. It is that we have forgotten our essential nature, who we are. When we remember the Knower, the ego has no claim or power over us.

Unchanging Allows you to Flow with the Changing

The situations in life are constantly changing. In order to be able to flow with all the changes you must be aware of that which never changes. You cannot make the things that are changing remain constant. Therefore, you will always suffer if you are concerned that things shouldn't change or wish they would stay the same. Instead, you need to tune into that which doesn't change. The inner being is unchanging. The Knower is unchanging. When you are established in that unchanging Knower, then the changes are experienced as the play the drama of life. You will find life exciting and challenging but never become dependent or feel that things should stay the same in order for you to remain happy.

Swami-ji said, "Your mind is Knowledgeable and ignorant simultaneously. Wait for a pause; in that pause, there is no mind; there is space. Then mind will take the order from God."

The human mind comes in the morning and goes in the evening; therefore, it is a changing substance. Therefore, it is only this relative knowledge that comes and goes. We are the unchanging reality, immortal, undying, and unchanging. Only a mistake comes that says, "I am the ego" or "I." Your body goes on acting, but you, the Knower, remain the same.

Your System Functions Without Your Control

Your thoughts come into your head not because you invite them. In the Spring, the leaves come, and the flowers bloom, but you have no control over them. All the sap goes to the roots in the Fall, and the leaves fall off. Again, you can't control these changes. In the same way your mind functions systematically due to your conditioning. This is not in your control. Swami-ji said," The Spring of your thoughts comes, and you have no control.

You should know who you are. You have come to grasp the knowledge that you are forever free." When the ego or "I" arrives, if you try to stop it, you will never be able to do it. Swami-ji said, "When the ego comes, you should become Pure Consciousness." Here, Swami-ji is saving us from trying to do something impossible. As he said, you can't become ego-less if you are ego. Therefore, the work is not to change or control your mind. Instead, you must know who you truly are, then ego doesn't exist.

Practices for the Week

1. Whenever you think, I am this body, mind, or ego, know instead that I am the sky, forever free.

2. Whenever you decide, pause and let the space guide you, not your mind.

3. When the ego comes in, bring in the knowledge of the Knower and be aware that you are the Knower, not the ego.

Lesson 17

All Human Beings are
Filled with Conflict

A fellow was visiting named Daniel. He is the nephew of a lady who has been living here for many years. It was exciting to watch him interact with Swami-ji. He is a very bright, articulate, and outgoing man, about 22 years old. He enjoyed interacting with everyone here, but certain concepts prevented him from benefiting from Guru's knowledge. Like many Western minds, he couldn't grasp the concept of Oneness. He observed that Swami-ji was separate from the rest of the people, and the people here depended on Swami-ji for Knowledge.

He had a very Western and dualistic viewpoint, so he felt that knowledge should only come from inside of him and not from someone else. This viewpoint echoed his great uncle's ideas, who didn't want his daughter (Daniel's aunt) to be here. Daniel said he was very independent and didn't need anyone. What was so interesting was the way Swami-ji spoke to him and how he answered his query.

Swami-ji said later that he never needs to convince anyone of anything by communicating with them. Swami-ji radiates the space and knowledge that he is. That is such a freeing idea. We don't have to convince anyone of our viewpoint or ideas. We are eternally free whether they believe us or not.

Swami-ji so cleverly directed the attention to Daniel's asking him a question. Swami-ji didn't need him to ask a question, so Daniel wanted to know something he didn't know. Swami-ji showed him that his concept or idea that he was separate, and all the knowledge had to come from his individual ego was erroneous.

Swami-ji later described this conflict of all human beings. They want to interact, participate, and experience joy, but their conditions from childhood and upbringing can limit them. There is this conflict between the true Self, which knows it is all One Being, and the ego, which feels it is individual. When one experiences Oneness in meditation, we know that Guru is not separate from me. Then, all the knowledge can be listened to and absorbed, and there is no separation within or without. It is all one space everywhere.

There is no Such Thing as Peace of Mind.

This statement is such an essential and revolutionary idea. How can there ever be peace of mind when the mind itself is not peaceful? Swami-ji said, "Why recommend to someone to have peace of mind? You don't tell the fire that it should become snow. Each person is peace-less, so he wants peace of mind." The very nature of the mind is that it is wavering and uneasy. Therefore, just making your mind quiet will never completely give you peace. If you identify as a mind and ego, your condition will be sometimes peaceful and sometimes peace-less. Then where is the peace?

When you meditate, you begin to observe that there is a You who is observing the mind. When you are in a deep sleep, you are peaceful; why? Because, at that time, your mind is absorbed in the space of your own being or Self. Then, the answer to being peaceful in the waking state is not making the mind peaceful but allowing the mind to be absorbed back into the Self, which is all peace. You are already peace. Then why do you have to make yourself peaceful? Instead, know who You are.

Peace is your underlying reality. It is always there behind all the thoughts, emotions, and experiences. Meditate and you will know the peace that you are and have always been. Swami-ji said, "The very being is forever at peace."

Can Meditation Be a Way of Escaping Problems?

A new lady was visiting from Canada. She has been meditating for five years and preparing herself to come. She said that sometimes she feels that by meditating, she is hiding from her life and problematic situations. She was asking Swami-ji for his guidance on this. Swami-ji responded by saying: "This is a false understanding. Meditation is a must to make the life good. You are not escaping from life. Rather, in meditation, you become strong and can deal with everything. There is no escape from life. Life is You, and in meditation, it becomes easy for a human being to know he is the life."

I have also heard people suggest this false idea over the years of my teaching meditation. Here, we can see how people are conditioned to believe that by using their minds, they will find solutions to their problems and that by surrendering their minds, they are copping out. This belief is backward. The very answered state only comes through meditation. When you are quiet and go within, you hear your inner voice which guides you in all situations. Then your life becomes an easy flow, and everything unfolds perfectly. Not necessarily according to your preferences or concepts but according to what is the highest for you.

This is another complex concept for many people to grasp. How do I get guidance from within? Some people may hear a voice speaking to them, but those who don't have a voice may think they have no guidance. This idea isn't the case for me and many others who do not hear a voice. For us, it is a natural flow with each situation rather than trying hard to figure out the best way or right decision. When we are open to the flow, it is like a voice, and we are moved in the right direction.

Swami-ji often gives this example when he says, "How do you know when you have to go to the bathroom or when you are finished?" He also described how, when you are asleep, everything in your system works perfectly. Therefore, the higher Self always guides us. We must be in tune with the flow. This means knowing that your ego and mind are tools to be used by the Self and that the Self is doing it all. Whenever you pause, and no thought is there, that is You. Whenever you have thought, that is the mind. Therefore, live in the pause and let the space guide you.

How Can I Deal with the Issues in my Life When I go Back to the West?

As soon as you think there is a separation and you have an issue, there is already no way to deal with the problem. The idea that this is an issue you must deal with will lead you astray. Why? Because then you have separated yourself from the whole. Swami-ji said, "You should be able to know that you are issue-less. What I call issue-less is I-less or ego-less. You do not have to deal with certain issues if you are infinite. Space is the totality where there is no matter."

The main point is that you are the free being, which means you are always free from any issue. Then you still might ask, "How do I live my life?" That is just the point; if you think you are living your life, you will always have complex issues. If, instead, you live from the perspective that it is all a show or dream and you are the best player in the drama that you call your life, then you will enjoy all the dramatic situations. You will always remain issue-less. Why do you want dramatic movies and intense suspense? Only because in that action is the joy of living.

Therefore, live your life with joy. You wouldn't like it if everything was perfect and always the same. The movie "Pleasantville" was such a great example of this. It was about a town where everything was perfect. There was no crime, no rain, no aging, and no death. The residents eventually saw that this colorless life was not what they truly desired. Even when the dramatic life was sometimes difficult, it was more meaningful than this fantasy or perfect world. Through this example, we can see that everything in the world is perfect.

Swami-ji once wrote this meaning to a beautiful ancient Sanskrit prayer, "There has never been any darkness. There has never been any mistake. There has never been anything wrong in this universe. There has been one objective field of relative existence. The creator sustainer and dissolver, Pure Existence, Pure Consciousness, and Pure Bliss."

Practices for The Week

1. Notice if there is a conflict within you between the true Self forever free and the ego self, that always wants to take charge. See if you can surrender this ignorance to the Self, ever free and pure. How do you surrender? Just be Pure Space like the sky.

2. Be aware that when communicating with someone, you need to convince them of something or your point of view. Just know you are a free being, needless. When you radiate from that space, they will come to know who they are, not separate from you. Then, you will be in harmony, even if the minds do not agree.

3. Take all the things you consider problems in your life and let them float away into the sky. Know you are issue-less. Everything will unfold perfectly from the space.

Lesson 18

How to Communicate from the Space

Someone asked a question about her ability to express herself. She said that whenever she gives a speech, her mind evaluates it. She wonders: "Was it a good speech? Did Swami-ji like it or not? Did she get her points across or not?" She wanted to know how she could feel free and not have this criticism going on in her mind. Swami-ji immediately brought attention to the Pure Awareness that we are. Meditating with this knowledge, we unfold a state where we know we are the space. Then, the intellect cannot be called you. The intellect takes the knowledge from the Pure Being.

Swami-ji said, "Then you begin to live in your awareness every moment; until then, you are a speaker who will say if a speech is good. When you realize the Being, as you are, you begin to know that you are no longer a body or an intellect who thinks such things." This problem continues only when you have not fully imbibed this highest awareness or purified the human system.

Swami-ji also gave an interesting and precise definition of the term *aparigraha,* which is from Patanjali, Paad II, in the section of the eight limbs. The term *aparigraha,* is usually defined as not possessing things. The meaning that Swami-ji gave is more transparent and more precise. He said, "*Aparigraha* is non-possession on the level of duality." From this, we can see how one can possess many things or have nothing, but it will not matter when you are stuck in dualistic thinking. If you don't own anything but feel separate and alone, that is not *aparigraha*. If you own many things but do not have a sense of attachment or possession to these things, then you are free.

This meaning recalls many situations that we have observed with Swami-ji. He was once a robbery victim, and afterward, he said it was terrific that the thief's family would now have a tape player to listen to music and a shawl to keep them warm. With the Vision of Oneness, it is all our own Self, so if someone else uses your things, that is also you, and you feel good. However, you still see what the thorns are and what roses are. So, you do not encourage or want people to steal. However, once it has happened, you can conclude to not upset yourself and to feel good for those who gained what they need. That is what is meant by not possessing duality.

Swami-ji also said that attachment begins with the I. If you wake up and think, "I woke up," then you will be attached. You will only be free from attachment and dualistic thinking when you wake up and know the very power or Self that woke me up and know that power that I am is not this individual body and mind.

Thoughts Keep Coming Like Your Hair Keeps Growing

When your thoughts came, you did not invite them. Therefore, why do you think that you can control them? This point is critical as it will free you from the entire realm of your thinking. If you take the time to observe the thoughts as an impartial witness, you will notice that thoughts come and then they go. If you wish them not to reach sometimes, they increase even more. If you want them to go, then sometimes they stay longer. Therefore, wishing or control is not the solution. Instead, understanding the nature of the mind and thoughts needs to be unfolded. Your hair grows, and you can let it stay long or cut it. You understand your hair's nature and don't try to control it as you know you can't.

In the same way, you know that your food is digesting, and you don't have direct control over how that is functioning. You have not ordered it to digest; it just happens. The very being you are is growing your hair, digesting your food, and giving you the power to think. You need to begin to recognize the natural functioning of your thoughts and the Pure Being who is directing it all.

Swami-ji said, "I say that the thoughts are not coming. Who told you that your head is yours? As long as your "I" arises in the morning and you think, "These are my thoughts, this is me," then all the problems of the human being will be yours; it just functions that way." He said, "All are Pure Being. All have originality in the *Aatma* (Self). The clear blue sky is the subtlest, and that is pure. What happened that infinite *aakash* (space) turned into this bulk (body) that I call me? We don't know. It just wanted to become a human being."

Is it Possible To be Desireless?

The very nature of the human being is desire. Desire is a must, as you need to desire food. Desirelessness does not mean you don't want to eat, drink, and conduct your life. The desire is not to go shopping or to Manali. The very nature of "I" is desire. To be free, you must know that you are always *aakash*

(Pure Space), then whatever the human being desires, who cares! Get it fulfilled if you can and remain free when you don't.

How to Deal with People That Bad Vibe You

Someone asked Swami-ji how you can feel easy when someone doesn't like you and is snubbing you or creating a bad vibe whenever they see you. Swami-ji so brilliantly answered. "When you don't have a *dwash* (aversion) channel, you do not feel *dwash.*" It is not possible to change the minds of others. Therefore, you will always fail if you think you will feel easy only when they stop what you don't like. The system works that way; however, like when you light a match, it creates fire. The human system feels it when someone treats you that way. The only escape is to know that you are like the *aakash* or space. Swords, words, or bad vibes can never cut or hurt the space.

The questioner went on to ask, "Does this happen gradually or all of a sudden that you can know you are *aakash?*" Swami-ji said, "We say it is gradual but if you light a match, it is not gradual. The sense of duality, or you become a person, or "I," is gradual. If you are a human being, all of this will continue. I have a system, but my system has been in that exercise that "I" is dissolved into *aakash.*" It is always interesting when Swami-ji explains how things are for him. Here, he is telling us that the human system still functions in this way; the only difference in his system is that he knows it is functioning and the body "I" he is not. He said, "I am the sky, but I have a human body."

The questioner asked, "Is it a choice that I have to conclude either I am a body or I am a sky?" Swami-ji said, "There is no choice as there is only *Sat, Chit, Aanand* (Pure Existence, Pure Consciousness, and Pure Bliss)." He informs us that as soon as this knowledge unfolds, it is automatic. You don't have to choose it. He said, "Why is it that you can retain the *dwash* or bad vibes that someone is sending you, but you don't retain the knowledge that you are Self, forever free and pure?" This point is enlightening as we can see how we are fixed or trained in the human system and how it functions.

Through our *sadhana* or practice, we begin to retain awareness, and the former feelings will be seen for what they are: passing waves in physical form. Then, the knowledge that we are space will be retained instead. Swami-ji then said so beautifully," When you realize your Self, you know that everyone is realized. Just like when you see the sunshine, it is the same sunshine everywhere."

Practices for the Week

1. Notice how your mind evaluates your speaking when you are in a group or giving a talk or speech. You can practice pausing and allowing the words to flow rather than always trying to say the right or best thing. You will be amazed at how much better you can express yourself when remaining open.

2. Observe your mind and thoughts. See that the thoughts come and then go. Know that these are not your thoughts. Imagine that they are happening in someone else's head. Do you worry about them then?

3. Notice when you are around someone, and you think that he doesn't like you. Remember, if you are sky, you don't have a channel to accept this disdain. The sky doesn't care when the birds eliminate in it. You can hear someone's voice criticizing you just like you hear a bird chirping. You don't have to give it meaning. They do not know any better; it is just their ego mechanism functioning. Their ego training functions that way, and they can't help it.

Lesson 19

Non-Doer-ship and Helping Others

When Swami-ji speaks of being the non-doer, people often conclude that this means that you do not act or that it is OK to remain inactive and wait until something from beyond moves you. That is not the true meaning of non-doer-ship. This day, he again explained the true meaning in a very concise way. He gave an example while holding a flower. He said, "I hold the rose and smell it, but doer-ship does not belong to the rose." When you woke up, did you wake yourself, or did the supreme reality wake you? Even when you don't use an alarm clock to wake up, you will wake up each morning.

Swami-ji said, "The one who wakes you up and who made you walk is like an infinite magnet, and you are like the iron filings. When your iron filings begin to move, you think you are moving, but the magnetic force is moving you. Each iron filing says, "I am going towards the north," but the magnet attracts you towards the North." Therefore, everything is perfect as the supreme power or source magnet always guides you.

The Problem with Words and Expression

If I say that I ate bread and jam, you may conclude that I ate baked bread, but I meant that I ate chapatis. Therefore, only the person who is expressing knows what they truly mean. The person hearing is always interpreting according to their concept. No wonder people have a hard time understanding each other and getting along. Swami-ji constantly says we are pure and free, but if you think and were told that you are a sinner and that for a human being to err is human, you will not understand what he means. The human being is filled with darkness and does not know his freedom and purity. But when the sun shines, the darkness will not remain.

In the same way, when the light of the highest awareness fills your being, you will not remain ignorant. Meditation will fill you with that light of the Self. Meditation doesn't mean sitting in silence; it means knowing who you are as Pure Space.

How to Truly Help Someone

A man living near the Ashram was visiting his mother in the States. She had been to India and attended satsang a few times. Her son was asking how he could help her. She has asked him to come as she is having trouble meditating due to her remorse because of her daughter's suicide, which happened two years ago.

Swami-ji immediately brought attention to the ineffective way her son believed he could help her. Swami-ji brought his attention to the fact that if he thinks of his mom as problematic, diseased, or incapable, he will be perpetuating the same thing that has always gone on. Swami-ji said, "Your mother is ajar (unborn), *amar* (immortal) and *avinaashi* (indestructible)." As long as her son keeps seeing her in the light of lacking something or needing something, all his efforts to help will fail. He has to see her as free and pure, and then she will become that.

This lady also wrote a letter to Swami-ji that he read in satsang. Her letter said that she was upset over her daughter's suicide as she felt that she should have been able to do something to save her. Swami-ji's response was terrific. He said, "You think you are the "I" who had her in your womb, and then she was born to you as your daughter, but really, she was always the blue space, and she was never yours. You are never the "I" that possesses something. Therefore, you are not the "I" who could save her. It is all God's doing which brought her back to her original abode. She is closer to you now because you can see her as the space she has always been."

Then he gave a beautiful P.S. to his letter. After pausing for a minute, he spoke as if he was a messenger and was speaking as her daughter, saying, "Mom, I am always with you as the blueness. I am there whenever you close your eyes; watch the blueness, and that is me." Guru-ji knows how to release us all from any sense of doer-ship or I-ership.

Overcoming Fear

The problem is that in the head of a human being, the sense of "I" appears. Therefore, the very attachment to the sense of "I" is the problem. When there is no sense of "I," such as when you are asleep, then there is no fear. When Swami-ji says, you are pure and free, what does that mean? If you think that the body is me, then you are not pure and free, as these are not qualities of the human body or machine. He is talking about that before the "I"; that is what you should call yourself.

Swami-ji said, "Daily you are snatched from that. I know that if you know that you are Pure Being, your fear will go away. If you let the seed grow, it will make a tree, but if you fry it, it will not. If your "I" is fried, it will not make you a person."

What Does it Mean to Practice This?

Swami-ji said so beautifully that one day, "One person's knowledge fills the whole Garden of Eden with love and knowledge. All of you are the sunlight; why would there be any darkness?" Practice does not mean you should strain yourself into repetitive poses or efforts, like lifting weights or working out in the gym.

We know that with physical exercise when there is a result in mind, such as getting stronger muscles or a smaller waist, you work every day to get stronger or lose inches. That is not what Swami-ji means by *abhiyas* or practice. He means that each time you sit to meditate or de-identify with your "I" and know you are Space, you have achieved the very result of your practice.

Therefore, practice is gaining the knowledge of who you are every time you do it. Yoga means union with the Self. You should also remember this when practicing Hatha Yoga, *Yog* or Union. You should practice in a way that each time you unite with the Self, rather than trying to perfect the poses or improve your body or mind, which is common in the West.

How to Deal with Headaches

Someone asked, "How should I view my machine (body) when I have a headache and it doesn't give me what I want." Swami-ji answered, "You should say that my body doesn't give me that which I can know that I am consciousness. The waves come in the lake of the same consciousness, and it is still all well. As long as you are identified, you will have a headache." Swami-ji pointed out that if you think you are your head, you will get stuck in it as it aches.

When you identify with Pure Consciousness, your head will have a sensation, but you are Pure consciousness. This lady then asked how I could identify with consciousness. Swami-ji raised a bowl and said, "What is this?" She said, "That is a bowl." Swami-ji said," How do you identify that with this? She said, "With consciousness." He explained that just like you know, this is a computer, and this is a tree; you can see that I am consciousness and not the table. I have a head, but in me is consciousness, and that I am. He said, "Consciousness will know the headache, and you will go to the hospital or a doctor to check it out."

Freedom from Self Doubt

The one who doubts is the one who says I woke up. The Pure Self has no doubt. Therefore, you must know who you are and who woke up. The mixture of the Pure Being with the Self will create doubt. Then, you must know how to sieve out the mixture. The mixture is of subject and object, and you want to be only the subject. Swami-ji said, "Then your attention should only be on the unchanging subject. Your mind is changing, and the Self is unchanging."

Revelation On Chapter Four of the Bhagavad Gita

That morning, Swami-ji was reading from the Bhagavad Gita and interpreting it from Sanskrit into Hindi. He was engaged in this project for a while. His son was writing Swami-ji's interpretation as he dictates it in Hindi, interpreting and commenting on the Sanskrit.

That morning, he said he was commenting on chapter four as no one has ever given the correct meaning. He was always making it more straightforward for everyone's understanding and the unfoldment of the true knowledge of the Gita. He has often said that the Bhagavad Gita has been around for ages, and all of India reads it, but still, those who read it aren't realizing the Self. Therefore, Swami-ji wrote a new scripture through his direct realization, which will unfold this state in its readers as the words are only limited to our understanding.

Guru must sieve out the true meaning and make it more transparent and precise so we can unfold this in our being. He has succeeded, and therefore, he is the guide to show those who have not. A book can never do this if you see only words printed on paper. Consequently, he is not telling us the word-for-word meaning but using language to draw attention to our source, which is forever pure and free.

The following is his revelation on Chapter Four as he expressed it that morning: Knowledge is given that a human being knows that he is the mind or intellect, as he has been told this and has accepted that he is his name by looking in the mirror. Then, he considers himself a human being and thinks that this whole collection of human beings could have never been if the Supreme Power had not been there. He knows the Supreme Power is doing everything.

Even the so-called mind, which receives all the thoughts, must not be something separate from the Supreme Power. If true, why should he call himself a mind, body, and doer? He no longer accepts this. He always knows that the Supreme Being is the reality. Such a person remains free while acting, interacting, eating, and drinking. He has come to know Supreme Reality is *Aatma* (the Self). Then, he does not incur sin because of his actions.

Practices for The Week

1. Ask yourself, "Who is waking me up in the morning? Who is digesting my food and growing my hair?" Then, you will be in touch with the Supreme Power doing it all. Know that the Supreme Power is the doer who allows your ego to function and even say, "I exist." Whenever you think something has been done right or wrong, just know that it is the supreme power doing it all, and you can remain free.

2. When someone shares a problem with you, do you sympathize and feel bad that they are suffering? See if you can adjust your perception and think they are pure and free. Then, you will know that you can best serve them by seeing their perfection rather than trying to fix the problem for them or dwelling on it.

3. When you practice hatha yoga or meditation, know that you are the result, forever pure and free, rather than hoping that this will be attained someday.

Lesson 20

The True Meaning of "Self Alone is Everywhere"

If the Self alone is everywhere, is the mind, ears, eyes, birds, trees, and everything all the Self? You can understand this through the essential meaning. You can make false conclusions if misunderstood. If it is all Self, I can do anything or go anywhere. I can eat the wrong food as that is the Self. You may also keep bad company as everyone is the Self. If you conclude that the body isn't the Self, why should I care for it or be concerned or bothered by it? These concepts or conclusions result from a false understanding of "Self alone is everywhere."

Swami-ji said, "The Self is all-permeating, all-pervasive, and the Self permeates all. Thus, all the forms are made from or are modifications of the same Self-material and are permeated by the Self." Therefore, it is said that "Self alone is everywhere. "Nothing could manifest without the power of the Self flowing through it. Once it has been made into its modification, that doesn't mean that even though it has the qualities of the Self, it is all unchanging Self.

The Self is unchanging and should never be compared with that which is changing. The intellect and mind constantly fluctuate and change, but the Self never changes. Therefore, although the Self permeates the mind and gives it its power to think, all thoughts are not unchanging and, thus, not the Self. They are modifications of the same force or power of the Self. Therefore, one can observe or know thoughts.

The very Knower who knows the thoughts is unchanging. Therefore, staying established in the Knower is recommended and not becoming mixed with the thoughts. Self also creates the dream state, but you do not act on or worry about the people or happenings in your dreams when you are in the waking state.

The main point here is to know that the Self, as the unchanging Being, is everywhere. All that changes are functioning through the power of the Self, but it is on the level of change; just like the dreams change, the waking state is also changing. Knower alone is everywhere, and the unchanging Knower is present through all the state of consciousness. The Knower knows where to place the body. Knower also knows what company is *satsang*, the highest awareness, and what company is of the mind. Then you will keep the highest company and only put the purest foods in your body because "Self alone is everywhere!"

Swami-ji said, "For the one who has realized, "Self alone is everywhere," for him there is no object. Self is neither subject nor object. It is independent. The knowledge or ability is of unchanging, this is to be added. Without this knowledge, one only knows what is changing. All the schools and psychologies focus on what is changing."

Living in the World with this Knowledge

Someone visiting from Canada said he is fine at the ashram, established in the unchanging, but when he goes to Canada, he gets caught in his mind again.

How can he live in the world more effectively with this knowledge? Swami-ji immediately said that this was a problem because the meaning of "the world" was not understood. The human mind has millions of *vrittis* (waves of perception or thoughts). When you are asleep, the world doesn't exist. Many people died in their sleep, and the world is still going on. In the waking state, you know that the world exists; in deep sleep, it does not exist.

Swami-ji said, "Now you have to find out what happened. The person asleep didn't die. If sleep takes place, then in the waking state, what changes? The waking state came instead of deep sleep, and deep sleep came instead of the waking state. But who is that who didn't change? Even though he is the same, the Being appears to be different.

People have attributed that there are two beings, but I say there is One." He then gave the example that the Being is forever free and pure; only the dress gets muddy or worn out. The Being cannot be compared with the dress, the body, or the world. He said, "You are working on it, but you are not yet convinced.

Therefore, you say that the rope is a snake or that the unchanging Being is the world." When you know you are the unchanging Being, pure and free, there is no separate world for you. You remain free while acting, interacting, performing, and playing. For you, the world and space are One reality.

Why is Meditation Not Enough and Satsang Essential?

I remember learning to meditate when I was nineteen. The system I learned didn't give me knowledge of the Self. The information about *vrittis* and de-identification was not included in the program. They just taught me a mantra and a technique without explaining how the system would work to unfold the highest awareness. Meditation was flat and ineffective without this vital link to my understanding of this process.

When we meditate, we experience the space of our own Being. If you didn't know what was happening in your meditation, then how would you know? You may feel peaceful and easy, but would you know how your mechanism was functioning to allow this to happen? Would you know how to live in the fourth state of consciousness throughout the day?

Without listening to the words of the Guru, either through these lessons, audio, his writings, or in satsang, the knowledge or the understanding of your system would not unfold. Then Meditation would only bring about part of the result. You need this continued guidance along the way, which is very important even when you become more advanced. Then, you do not become misguided or waste your time with mistaken understanding.

Swami-ji said, "Without hearing, your knowledge would have never been achieved. Something in the human system covers the knowledge. It opens when you hear about it; when you don't, it stays covered. The dross disappears from the ears through hearing, and knowledge is uncovered." To remove this covering one needs satsang (company of the truth). To avoid being affected by the human system, which has specific channels, some of which one is unaware of, you must hear this knowledge and assimilate it.

Swami-ji said, "Meditation gives you power, but it does not give you knowledge. Many people meditate their whole life, but the knowledge has not yet arrived. The human machine has to be studied thoroughly; it is the most defective machine, yet it is effective because you can realize the knowledge." As the attachment to the "I" is the most subtle, as it is the very waking state, you must hear about how "I" functions and study it. Then, you will come to know the "I" as the space, pure and free. Swami-ji beautifully said, "Human consciousness is higher than the sky because the sky can't know us."

Practices for The Week

1. Notice what concepts you may have about the meaning of "Self alone is everywhere." Do you use it to justify some of what you do, even though you know they are not helpful? Do you not take that good care of your body because you are peaceful in meditation and don't want to bother? Stop and remember the true meaning of "Self alone is everywhere. " It means you are that Self. Therefore, take care of yourself as it is your temple to achieve this awareness of the Self.

2. Notice when you get up in the morning and the intellect says, "I woke up into this world." Reflect on this moment: the world is your creation in the waking state. It wasn't there for you when you were asleep, but you were alive. Therefore, you are that Being before waking up, not the "I" that falsely believes, "I woke up." You are the unchanging Being permeating both sleep and waking state. You are forever Pure and Free!

3. Reread all the lessons and listen to what Swami-ji says. This knowledge of the Self will bring about

the state of freedom and purity in all the situations in the world. Attend regular satsang, listen to Shree's audios online, or create satsang by reading and discussing these lessons with your friends.

Lesson 21

Realization Doesn't Mean that you Become Like a Rock or that you Suppress your Feelings

There is often a misunderstanding that some people have about the Self-realized state. It is sometimes compared to deep sleep, where you have no feelings. Then, you may conclude that it is a state devoid of feelings. Swami-ji has often told us that this is not correct. He has sometimes said that he feels everything; he is one with everyone: a child crying on the road, someone sad in the room, and a worker unhappy about his life. How can a realized being feel all this and always remain in freedom and delight?

Swami-ji said, "All of your thoughts and experiences should give you the result that you feel and know that *Aatma*, the Self, the Pure Being, is all there is. Then why should you be devoid of the experiences? If someone is high in celebrating their birthday, then shouldn't we be high? If someone is in pain, we must take them to the doctor. Yet the *Aatma*, the Self, remains forever free and pure."

This may be a complex state to comprehend. However, through the practice of meditation, you will reach there. When you are established in your true nature, your body feels, but you, the true "I" or Self, remain always unaffected. Your body is never like a rock. You need to feel the thorn in your foot to take it out. Yet simultaneously, you know that you are not limited to the body. You will experience this free state as your *saadhana* progresses.

Everything is Happening for Your Good

Someone going to visit her family in the U.S. asked how she can remain free with the people she will have to be involved with when she is in the West. She will be with her family members and friends who do not have this knowledge and understanding. Swami-ji beautifully said to her, "One thing, you should always conclude that everything is happening for your good and your evolution. Remember my words that you are pure and free and perfect."

Swami-ji continued to talk about the power and effect of this knowledge. He said that it looks like he is only talking to a small group of people here in the Himalayas, but his voice, the voice of the highest expression, is going out into space, and so much improvement is happening in the world. He reminded us, what he had said over twenty years ago; when meditation was not a very popular practice with the mainstream society, that one day meditation will be on the lips and tongues of every intelligent person. Now we see that this has happened. Therefore, one should never underestimate the power and effect of our satsang and share in this highest awareness.

Non-Doer Doesn't Mean Not Doing Anything

Someone had asked Swami-ji how to be active but remain free of the ego that believes it is the doer. Swami-ji said that you think you are the non-doer when you aren't acting and that if you are doing, you become ego. Even when you sit quietly, you are doing something; thinking or just sitting is an action. A person is born with the need for action. When he hasn't been given the knowledge of the Self, he will act only from duality and ego identity. Yet he is given the power when he receives the knowledge to remove the *avidya* (ignorance) and become knowledgeable.

Meditation is meant to unfold the fourth state of consciousness. Swami-ji said, "When you are meditating, the most strenuous work, people will say you aren't doing anything, so you are a non-doer. The meaning of non-doers-hip is the sky. The sky means pure and free. People begin to think, 'I am caught.' Why is the child not caught? He says or does anything because he doesn't have the sense of I am this "I" or this person. If this sense of 'I' was not in the beginning and it was created, then it is not permanent. It is finite if this 'I' is treated as the body. If this 'I' is treated as the sky, it is infinite. Those who have not yet achieved *aatma gyaan* (knowledge of the Self), either performing or not performing actions, will remain worried."

God is Intelligence

Swami-ji put up a sign in the satsang hall that said, "Engagement for Ability Development." He made the point that we are researchers studying our own minds and systems to gain the ability to realize our fullest potential, the Vision of Oneness. The child feels defeated from the beginning of childhood. He must go to school and stay still but wants to play. He isn't given the knowledge that he is pure and free. Who needs this knowledge? The one who feels bound. There must be someone to give it to him. The Guru is the head researcher. You must get into the research on how to free human beings.

The problem is not with society; society will never be fixed unless we get to the root cause. The root should be firm and tuned into its originality. There are wars because people are afraid of death. Swami-ji said, "A good thinker is the one who knows the source of life. The blueness has come to your heart. Blueness is the sky, and that you are. You have to break the limits of the questions and make them limitless space."

Through meditation, you bring out your intelligence. Then, you will know when your mind comes in and what the very source of your mind is, which is the blueness. Swami-ji said, "You should not mind when you come to your thinking level. At the source, your intelligence becomes unlimited. Intelligence means turned into the source. God is intelligence."

Freedom is Not an Emotion

Swami-ji said, "Emotions start in the brain and penetrate every cell." When a mosquito bites your ear, the ear doesn't feel it. The sensation goes to the brain, and then you feel it. In the same way, when your body feels an emotion, it is processed through the brain and nervous system. Therefore, emotions are material substances. They are whirling all the time because of the situations.

When you love someone and they go away, you will have a flood of emotions. Because emotions are part of the body, the body will then become weak. Your emotions will say, "I am not pure, and I am not free." If you want to go beyond them, use your present awareness that the Self is finer than the sky and permeates the body. That awareness will counteract the emotions in the body. Swami-ji said, "The whole will work; the heart will not work."

Seeing Light in Meditation

To understand what meditation is, Swami-ji said that they don't say meditation is as simple as you are. You must ask whom do you call you? Then add the unchanging to the changing intellect. When you close your eyes, that is You." He then went on to explain what the meditative state is. He said, "They say we meditate to see the light. You have already seen the sun's light; why would you want to see the light when you close your eyes? This blueness permeates even the white light.

This insight dispels one of the biggest misconceptions about meditation. Some people think they should see things in meditation, such as images or lights. Seeing things in your meditation shows that you are still on the level of the mind. For you to see or perceive anything, you have to use your mind. Therefore, whenever you see things in your meditation, although you might be going into deeper levels of your mind, you are functioning on the mind level.

When you experience bliss in your mediation, this is still not the deepest level. Even bliss is on the level of experience unless it is the bliss of the Self, which is unchanging. That bliss is devoid of feelings and is pure consciousness. When you are left alone as the pure unchanging being, then you are, as you are.

What Does Krishna Mean When He Says, "Think of Me all The Time"

Someone expressed that she was studying a verse in the Gita in which Krishna says to Arjun that you should think of me all the time. She asked, "Swami-ji, what does it mean to think of Krishna?" Swami-ji said, "It should say instead, know me all the time."

Here he is making the distinction that one can think about something, but that is still on the level of the mind. When you know Krishna, you know the space, unchanging being.

Then Swami-ji asked this person what she meant by the word "think." She said, "When I think of someone, then it is of another." Swami-ji said," When you think of others, you can't think of others without you." He then explained how steeped the human being is in this sense of otherness or duality. Yes, without You, you can't even think. Without consciousness, which is oneness, you can't think clearly or unclearly.

He pointed out that you can't think clearly if you are in *avidya* (ignorance of the Self). You have to know who "I" is and what attaining Me means, then you can think clearly. He then showed her how she superimposes the Self on the mind and body and expects the mind and body to remain unchanging as the Self is unchanging. This was a critical point. When one comes to know they are unchanging Self, then an expectation can be created that the mind should think clearly, the body should not fail me. This is not correct.

The Self remains unchanging no matter what happens in the body and the mind. The body and mind will continually change. Therefore, if your mind is agitated or your body is unhealthy, that has nothing to do with the Self, as the Self hasn't changed. You can view your body and mind as if it belongs to someone else. Then it would not trouble you. You then take care of your body as you would take care of anyone else living with you, but you don't get troubled by it. You also don't expect it to be as perfect as You; the Self is pure, free, and always perfect.

Swami-ji said, "When you say, "I feel pain," you mean I, the mind." The Self doesn't feel pain, as it is unchanging.

Practices for the Week

Notice when an emotion comes or when physical pain arises. Does it get processed by your brain? Is the Knower of the emotion or pain affected? Think about this body as if it belongs to someone else. Would you then feel it in the same way? Remain the uninvolved Knower.

2. Whenever things don't go according to your preferences, remind yourself that it is all happening for your evolution. You are always pure, free, and perfect.

3. When you arise in the morning, observe the first sense of "I" am arising. Who were you before the "I" arose? Then, notice who compels you to move. Notice that you are there before the "I." When the mind compels you to move, who moves you? Even though the mind thinks you are moving, you don't move when you dream.

4. Know that we are all engaged in ability development. When you become a good researcher of your own system, you gain the ability to remember the Self and space as who you are always.

Lesson 22

I Get Caught Up with Memories that I Don't Like

Someone was expressing that when she has bad memories from the past, she gets identified with them and suffers. Swami-ji said, "You have not practiced that you are the one who never gets caught. You are calling yourself the "I" who can get caught." Here, Swami-ji explains that when you say, "I get caught," you must know who gets caught. It is the mind that gets caught. If the mind gets caught and you think you are the mind, then and only then will you get caught. Your reality is not the mind because you are the seer of the mind. The seer is different from what you are seeing.

Swami-ji said: "If you are the one who is seeing, let the mind be caught; you are not caught." With what agency do you feel? You feel because the brain processes the information. When a mosquito bites the ear, your ear doesn't feel the pain alone without the brain or mind sensing the pain. An ear not connected to your brain or mind would not feel pain. When you say, 'I feel pain,' you have called it 'I," the mind. The Knower has become mixed with the mind because you have so rigidly said you are mind.

This type of identification is called the *sanyog* or the mixture state. When somebody else feels pain, you are not in *sanyog,* you do not feel it, but you may sympathize with them. In the same way, when you are de-identified with your mind, you do not feel the

227

pain. Only the brain or mind can feel it, not You, the Self, or the Knower.

How to Deal with Two Different Opinions

The sky does not change because a man is born. One must find the unchanging source. Man is born with the sense of duality. It is not your fault as it has been constructed that way. You see a person, and you call it other. We must find out how this duality creates the problem. Before you were born, everything was all right. What happens to human beings as soon as they come to earth? As soon as you come on earth, you will be in duality. If you know it is duality and you do not like it, then you are inspired to find out how this duality will not happen.

Swami-ji asked, "What happens when the duality appears?" The questioner answered, "Uneasiness." Every human thinks that when duality appears because of things, forms, and seeing others, they should accept it. Desire appears because of ignorance of yourself as eternal. When that is lost, then uneasiness comes. Everyone is seeking liberation from this. You are not a human being. You are liberation, freedom, and purity. Swami-ji asked, "Who is it within your body that says freedom and liberation is not me?"

Before uneasiness was there, you were not uneasy; you were pure and free. A person with a cement bag on their back is the same person. If uneasiness is riding on your back, like a cement bag, then you think, "I am uneasy," but really, uneasiness is superimposed on you. You don't say, "I am," you say, "I am uneasy." Duality means that which you are not and begin to call "I". If the "I" is bound, it will try to be free wherever it goes. When you know you are free, you will have favorable and loving relation-ships. Millions of *vrittis* (waves of perception or thoughts) will pass but you remain unmoved, for-ever free and pure.

Should I Watch in Meditation or Should I Go for Space or Thoughtlessness?

Someone said that he felt he could watch whatever was happening in his meditation or try to experience space or thoughtlessness. He wanted to know which is preferable. Swami-ji answered: "As space is eve-rywhere, the right attitude is that whatever is hap-pening is the state of perfection. If you think that no thoughts should come, that is correct. If thoughts come, that is also correct. Suppose you want to make something happen that is correct. What is that which is not the space? Who is saying there should be thoughtlessness or thoughts? That is you. Its name is perfection.

Perfection means You. If you think you are not per-fect, but you know you are perfection, it is you. Know this fact: there is absolutely no one else other than You. Who is that who wants this? I- that 'I' is one without a second, totally united. To remove this division is the only work."

That was such a meaningful answer. We must know that whatever thoughts come while meditating are perfect. The very nature of the mind is that it gener-ates thoughts. If you think to have no thoughts or to watch, those are also thoughts. As soon as you think that the thoughts should be different than they are and you believe that thought, you miss the underlying perfection, which is forever unchanging.

The thoughts never bother the meditator. They know that the thought is only a modification of the same consciousness, which is always free from the thought. Just like the wave in the ocean is the same ocean water. We can call it a wave, or we can call it water. We can call it a thought, a wave of perception, or Pure Consciousness, Space itself.

Definition of Consciousness

A scientist who lives in Kullu wanted to correspond with other scientists on the internet. He asked Swami-ji how he could define consciousness when speaking to other scientists. Swami-ji replied: "What made you ask? That is consciousness. You are saying, 'I am a conscious being,' but you are ignoring its source, which is consciousness pure. If you see two, you are not grasping pure consciousness.

Pure consciousness never sees two, consciousness or material, birth or death. When you meditate, you are no longer a human being trying to perceive consciousness. You are a conscious being; you are not dead material. The definition of pure consciousness is eternal existence."

Swami-ji was leading the attention to the direct experience of the meaning of consciousness, rather then using the mind to make up another term. Consciousness is the direct experience that one has in meditation. Even though the mind is not functioning, you are still alive when you are in deep sleep. If someone calls your name loud enough, you will awaken. Who is it that heard?

The very consciousness was present. You were still breathing, and all your bodily functions were working even though your mind was asleep. Therefore, consciousness you are and you are always present. To make this more evident, Swami-ji has called it the Knower. The Knower is present in all the states: dream, deep sleep, waking, and meditative. That Knower is Pure Consciousness or Eternal Existence.

Why Did God or Pure Consciousness Create Separation or Duality

We have heard that God or *Aatma* created this world. Swami-ji says: "God has never created this world. This world is only due to the waking state. God has not created the world of politics and fighting. People have created a concept of God to escape this mess. People who are confronted with suffering say, 'It is the soul or God or spirit who likes to create this to suffer and then go to the place not to suffer.

The waking state being created bondage. That is the human species. There is no such thing as God wanting to plan himself to be a pig. When you see flowers, you say God created this nice world, but you don't like to say he created the bugs and pollution. It is not the God who created this; it is a human being, and human beings created God. Why does a human being wish to remain free? People will say it is God's wish as if God is bound."

This brilliant and revolutionary idea is so profound because it answers the question many people ask, "If there is a God, why did he create suffering?" Swami-ji brings in the knowledge that God is Pure Consciousness, totally free and pure. It is the waking state being who begins to say, "I am separate from God," that creates separations, duality, wars, etc. Therefore, when one is tuned into God Consciousness, one is always at peace.

How to be Free from Attachment

Swami-ji said, "Your attachment should be *veet raag* (victory over attachment). Anything you see is a thing, form, or person. If you think they are permanent, you will have *raag* for them." Patanjali says you must have *vairaagya*. You only think that the things, forms, objects, and persons will give you permanent happiness because you are a victim of your senses. *Vairaagya* is the knowledge of how to lead this human life with the help of the senses.

You must know *kaivalya* (state of unity). You were never anything else but Pure Being. *Agyaan* or ignorance is when you forget your immortal Self and begin to attach to the things and forms you think will give you true happiness. When you don't lack anything and know your true nature, totally fulfilled, then you are said to be *veet raag*. Swami-ji said, "*Raag* means everything is essential, but in the light of death, what is essential?"

Practices for the Week

1. Here are a few quotes from Swami-ji that you can practice repeating to yourself throughout the day. They will bring awareness and inspiration. It is the mind that gets caught and not me. Whatever thought I think, it is okay. I am not that thought.

2. Every day, when you wake up until you sleep, you should not make your day terrible. You can know just today; you have known it and now must hold it. Your reality was not born. You can see people changing and dying but you are unchanging. Actors

on the stage aren't happy or unhappy. You can also be either one so why not act happy. When you wake up in the morning repeat the mantra. Decide that you will remember throughout the day your experience of Pure Consciousness that was unmoved and unaffected the entire night you were asleep.

3. Notice who or what you are attached to. Tell yourself that it is not the person or thing that you really need. It is the lack of your inner sense of satisfaction and fulfillment that makes you falsely believe you need someone or something else. Know that you are forever pure and free and will always be.

Epilogue

This book was designed to answer many possible questions that can arise when meditating and practicing unfolding a direct awakening in meditation. Numerous practical situations and challenges can arise. As we all are already realized, you cannot fail in pursuing your wishes to be Self-realized. However, you can fall into forgetfulness and remain stuck at any level.

This forgetfulness can occur even for those who have practiced for many decades. The human condition is so rampant and ingrained that we need constant reminders. It is like a tiny ant trying to eat the whole mountain. So, never feel bad about yourself or what you have achieved. Even a little progress towards knowing the truth is a great gift you can give yourself. The human incarnation is the highest of all species as we can realize our true Self. Knowing this, you should always take the best care, love, and appreciate yourself.

After reading this book, you can pick it up again whenever you feel like you have lost this space or become caught in forgetfulness of your true Self. Whenever you believe only in the thoughts in your mind and feelings in your body, you can read one passage to transform your limited mental awareness to the fullness of space awareness. When I was reading through this book because it contained this knowledge, it automatically shifted my attention to meditative awareness, the direct awakening.

You can also practice the weekly exercises to re-member who you are and get reinspired. After reading this book, I hope you meditate on your true nature and know it completely. I hope you become free from any-thing holding you back and can accept and know that it will pass as it changes, and you, the Self, are unchanging, Pure, Free, and Forever!

Blessed you are to have known this and to abide in its glory.

About the Author

Sherrie Wade, M.A. (Chaytna Shree or Shree)

Shree received her master's degree in counseling psychology and had practiced in Florida for many years as a licensed therapist (#3015). She has come to realize that the peaceful meditative state is our true nature. She speaks and writes with clarity and wisdom about how one can unfold this awareness and transform one's life. She is a certified meditation instructor from the International Meditation Institute, Himalayas, India, where she spent over twenty years in self-inquiry and study with her Guru-ji, Swami Shyam.

Shree has taught meditation since 1985 and is now known as a teacher of teachers and counselor specializing in stress management and meditation. She is certified by the National Board of Certified Counselors.

Shree was the Director of The Meditation Center in Delray Beach, Florida, where she developed and conducted Transformation Meditation Teacher Training and evolved the home-study programs. The links to register are on her website www.transformationmeditation.com. She has written articles for numerous newspapers and magazines and was a featured columnist for several years. She is the author of several books and has audios and courses on meditation apps, as well as podcasts on many channels.

Works by Shree

Home Study Manuals

- Doubt Free Meditation Foundation Series
- Transformation Meditation Teacher Training

Books and Audios:

- Love's Eternal Space, Enlightening Poetry, book
- Knowingness Meditation: Enlightenment is Now, book
- Direct Awakening in Meditation: From Mindfulness to Knowingness, book
- Infinite Peace Meditation, audio
- Transformation Meditation Teacher Training, audio

Meditation Recording and Courses on Insight-timer and Aura Health Meditation Apps and Podcasts:

- Transformation Meditation Teacher Training
- Satsang Podcasts (140 recordings) on many podcast channels
- Eight Steps to Self Realization, series of eight audio recordings
- Praan Chintan: The Power of Breathwork Audio Course
- Yoga Sutras of Patanjali: Samaadhi Paad - Meditation for Self Realization Course with book and audio

Contact:

- www.transformationmeditation.com
- www.transformedu.com
- shree@transformationmeditation.com

Made in United States
Troutdale, OR
05/07/2025